A TREATISE
ON POETRY

CZESLAW MILOSZ

TRANSLATED BY THE AUTHOR
AND ROBERT HASS

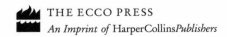

THE ECCO PRESS
An Imprint of HarperCollins*Publishers*

HarperCollins books may be purchased for educational, business, or sales promotional use. For information please write: Special Markets Department, HarperCollins Publishers, Inc., 10 East 53rd Street, New York, NY 10022.

FIRST EDITION

Designed by Cassandra J. Pappas

Library of Congress Cataloging-in-Publication Data
Milosz, Czeslaw.
    [Traktat poetycki. English]
    A treatise on poetry / Czeslaw Milosz; translated by Robert Hass.
        p. cm.
    ISBN 0-06-018524-4
        I. Hass, Robert. II. Title.
    PG7158.M553 T6913 2001
    891.8'517—dc21   00-047694

01 02 03 04 05 RRD 10 9 8 7 6 5 4 3 2 1

Contents

TRANSLATOR'S NOTE

CZESLAW MILOSZ'S REMARKABLE *A Treatise on Poetry* was begun in the winter of 1955 and finished in the spring of 1956. The first three parts were printed in the June 1956 issue of the émigré journal *Kultura.* "Natura" appeared in December 1956. The first section of the poem, "Beautiful Times," describes Kraków and Polish culture at the turn of the nineteenth century. The second section, "The Capital," describes Warsaw and makes an assessment—almost poet by poet—of the state of Polish poetry in the first three or four decades of the century, particularly of its failure to account for the reality that overwhelmed that city. The third section, "The Spirit of History," on the war years, is a meditation on the nature of history, on language, and on raw force. It begins like this:

> When the gold paint flakes from the arms of sculptures,
> When the letter falls out of the book of laws,
> Then consciousness is naked as an eye.

When the pages of books fall in fiery scraps
Onto smashed leaves and twisted metal,
The tree of good and evil is stripped bare.

The fourth section, "Natura," makes a startling leap. The war is over. The narrator is sitting in a boat on a lake in northern Pennsylvania, waiting for a vision from the books of his childhood: a hoped-for glimpse of the American beaver. It is a meditation on nature, on Europe and America, and on the role of the poet in the postwar world. Some of the many cultural references in the poem are tracked in a new edition of the *Treatise* which appeared recently in Poland accompanied by the author's own notes on the poem, forty years after the fact. They have been translated and somewhat revised here for the interest of English-language readers.

A word on form: The poem is written in a rather strict meter. The English equivalent would probably be a plain, regular, and forceful blank verse. It also breaks from time to time into more lyric forms. In "Natura," for example, there are the small song "Inside the Rose"; "O City," a set of prophetic rhymed quatrains that carry echoes of the romantic and apocalyptic style of nineteenth-century Polish poetry; and an old-fashioned ode to the month of October which, in 1955–1956, glints with multiple ironies, since October was in People's Poland the occasion for public celebrations of the Russian Revolution. To give some sense of the surprise of these forms, it would have been desirable to find English equivalents. But because their tone is often complex and because they have philosophical bearing in the poem, it also seemed desirable to hew fairly closely to the literal meaning, at least in this first English translation. In general we have tried to suggest, without being bound to, an English pentameter. And in the lyrics, we have for the most part taken Vladimir Nabokov's advice: "Better a crude word-for-word translation than the prettiest paraphrase."

A Treatise
on Poetry

First, plain speech in the mother tongue.
Hearing it you should be able to see,
As if in a flash of summer lightning,
Apple trees, a river, the bend of a road.

And it should contain more than images.
Singsong lured it into being,
Melody, a daydream. Defenseless,
It was bypassed by the dry, sharp world.

You often ask yourself why you feel shame
Whenever you look through a book of poems.
As if the author, for reasons unclear to you,
Addressed the worst side of your nature,
Pushing thought aside, cheating thought.

Poetry, seasoned with satire, clowning,
Jokes, still knows how to please.
Then its excellence is much admired.
But serious combat, where life is at stake,
Is fought in prose. It was not always so.

And our regret has remained unconfessed.
Novels and essays serve but will not last.
One clear stanza can take more weight
Than a whole wagon of elaborate prose.

PART ONE

BEAUTIFUL TIMES

Kraków 1900–1914

I. BEAUTIFUL TIMES

Cabbies were dozing by St. Mary's tower.
Kraków was tiny as a painted egg
Just taken from a pot of dye on Easter.
In their black capes poets strolled the streets.
Nobody remembers their names today,
And yet their hands were real once,
And their cufflinks gleamed above a table.
An *Ober* brings the paper on a stick
And coffee, then passes away like them
Without a name. Muses, Rachels in trailing shawls,
Put tongues to lips while pinning up their braids.
The pin lies with their daughters' ashes now,
Or in a glass case next to mute seashells
And a glass lily. Angels of Art Nouveau
In the dark WC's of their parents' homes,
Meditating on the link between sex and the soul,
Went to Vienna for migraines and the blues
(Dr. Freud, I hear, is also from Galicia),
And Anna Csilag grew her long, long hair.
The hussars' tunics were trimmed out with braid.
News of the emperor spread through mountain villages.
Someone had seen his carriage in the valley.

This is our beginning. Useless to deny it.
Useless to recall a distant golden age.

We have to accept and take as our own
The mustache with pomade, the bowler hat acock.
Also the jingle of a tombac watch chain.
It's ours, the worker's song, the mug of beer
In factory towns black as heavy cloth.
The match struck at dawn and the twelve hours
Labor to make wealth and progress out of smoke.

Lament, Europe! And wait for a *Schiffskarte*.
On a December evening in the port at Rotterdam
A ship full of immigrants stands silent
Under the frozen masts like snow-clad firs.
A chorus, or litany, breaks from below deck
In some peasant, Slovenian or Polish, dialect.
A pianola, hit by a bullet, begins to play.
A quardrille in a saloon drives the wild couples,
And she, fat, red-haired, snapping her garter,
In fluffy slippers, her thighs sprawling
Waits on a throne, she, mystery,
For traveling salesmen of Salvarsan and condoms.

This is our beginning. A cinematograph:
Max Linder leads a cow and falls down flat.
In open-air cafés lamps shine through the leaves.
A women's orchestra blows into trombones.

Till from hands, jeweled rings, lilac corsets,
From the ashes of cigars, it all unwinds, meanders

Through forests, lowlands, mountains, plains—
The command "*Vorwarts!*" "*En avant!*" "*Allez!*"

There are our hearts, sprinkled with quicklime
On empty fields that have been licked by flame.
And nobody knew why it suddenly ended,
—A pianola played—progress and wealth.

Our style, unpleasant to say it, was born there.
The sound of a lyre from a garret window
Hums in the dawn above a *Tingeltangel*,
The song as ethereal as the creaking stars,
Not needed by tradesmen and their wives, not needed
By the peasant farmers in a mountain village,
A pure thing, against the sad affairs of earth.
Pure, forbidden the use of certain words:
Toilet, telephone, ticket, ass, money.

A muse with long hair learns to read
In the dark toilet of her parents' home
And knows already what is not poetry,
Which is only a mood and a breeze. It dwells
In three dots, followed by a comma.

It flows and waves, ineffable. A stand-in
For religion, and such it will remain.
The breath of normal syntax will be banned:

"Eh, journalism. Let them write in prose."
Then, in the schools of a new avant-garde,
They will call this old injunction a discovery.
Not all poets vanished without a trace.
Kasprowicz roared, tore at the silken tethers
Yet could not break them: they were invisible.
And not tethers, they were more like bats
Sucking the blood out of speech on the fly.
Leopold Staff was the color of honey.
He praised witches, gnomes, and the rains of spring.
His praise was as if in a world of as if.
As to Leśmian, he drew his own conclusions:
If it's all a dream, let's dream it to the bottom.

In Kraków, on a narrow little street,
Two boys lived not far from one another.
When one of them walked to St. Anne's school,
He saw the other playing in the sand.
They had different fates, different fames.
For the sailor oceans, vast, incomprehensible,
Islands where naked tribes sounded a conch
Beyond a coral reef. The moment still exists
When, in a deserted street, in humid Brussels,
He walked slowly up the marble stairs
And pushed a bell marked by the letter S,
The Anonymous Society, listened to the silence,

Entered. Two women, knitting, pulled at threads—
They seemed to him Parcae—, then put away
Their skeins and gestured toward a door,
Behind which rose the managing director,
Also anonymous, to shake his hand.
It was in this way that Joseph Conrad
Came to captain a steamer on the Congo,
As was fated. For those who would hear it,
His tale of a jungle river was a warning:
One of the civilizers, a madman named Kurtz,
A gatherer of ivory stained with blood,
Scribbled in the margin of his report
On the Light of Culture: "The horror." And climbed
Into the twentieth century.
                                        Meanwhile
In a Krakóvian village, peasant costumes,
Wedding dances until daybreak to the tune
Of a double bass, also a puppet theater,
The same for centuries. Indomitable Wyspiański
Dreamed of a national theater, as in Greece.
He couldn't overcome the contradiction.
His medium deformed his vision and our speech.
It would make us prisoners of history,
Not persons, traces of persons, on a seal
Stamped only with the style of a time.
Wyspiański has not been of help to us.

As heritage we received another monument:
Conceived as a joke, not for any glory,
As much of the language as a street song,
A thumbing of the nose at abstract thought.
A pity it's a trifle: *Little Words* by Boy.
That day fades. Someone has lit the candles.
On Oleandry field the locks of the carbines
Don't click anymore, the plain is empty.
The aesthetes in infantry boots have departed.
Their hair has been swept from the barber's floor.
Fog and a smell of smoke hang about the place.

And she, she wears a lilac-colored veil.
By candlelight she puts her fingers to the keys
And while the doctor fills glasses with liqueur
She sings an air that seems to come from nowhere:

The laughter in cafés
Echoes about a hero's grave.

PART TWO

The Capital

Warsaw, 1918–1939

II. THE CAPITAL

You, alien city on a dusty plain,
Under the cupola of the Orthodox cathedral,
Your music was the fifes of regiments,
The Cavalry Guard was your soldier of soldiers,
From a droshky rings a lewd Caucasian ditty.
Thus one should begin an ode to you, Warsaw,
To your grief and debauchery and misery.
A street vendor, hands clumsy with cold,
Measures out a peck of sunflower seeds.
An ensign elopes with a railwayman's daughter.
He will make her a princess in Elisavetgrad.

At Czerniakowski Street, at Górna and Wola,
Black Mary carouses in the humming dives.
Upstairs she lifts a muslin skirt with frills.

And you are ruled, City, from a citadel.
Cossack horses prick their ears at the echo
Of a song: "Red banners wave above the thrones."

You have enough administering a province.
You, an amusement park on the Vistula,
How could you become the capital of a state
Crowded with refugees from the Ukraine

Peddling jewels from their manors near Odessa?
A saber, rifles from French army surplus,
These will have to serve you in your battles.
They are striking against you—ridiculous—
On the London docks and in enlightened Prague.

And so volunteers in the propaganda offices
Write articles about the onslaught from the East.
They don't know that, one day, harsh brasses will play
The "Internationale" above their graves.

Yet you exist. With your blackened ghetto,
The somnolent anger of your unemployed,
Your womens' tears and their prewar shawls.

For years Piłsudski paced in the Belvedere.
He could never believe in permanence.
And would say again: "They will attack us."
Who? He pointed to the East, the West.
"I've stopped the wheel of history a moment."

Morning glories will sprout from spots of blood.
Where wheat is kneeling, boulevards will rise.
And a generation will ask how that moment felt.

Till not one stone, O city, remains
Upon a stone, and you too will pass away.

Flame will consume the painted history.
Your memory will become a dug-up coin.
And for your disasters this is your reward:
As a sign that language only is your home,
Your ramparts will be built by poets.

A poet needs, first, to issue from good stock,
To have a saintly tzaddic in his lineage.
His parents, of course, would have read Lassalle,
Believed in progress and lieder from Berlin.
Refinement distills itself slowly. Some
Came from much less fancy folk, from gentry
Or burghers, even from a German in a nightcap.

Noisy at the Picadore they did not guess
That laurels sometimes have a bitter taste.
Tuwim dilated his nostrils when reciting,
Shouted "*Ça ira!*" in Grodno or Tykocin,
And set the crowd of native youth trembling
At a sound belated by a hundred years.
He would meet his admirers who survived
Years later at a ball for the Security Police,
Which brought a fiery circle to its close:
The ball at the Senator goes on and on.
Lechoń-Herostrates trampled on the past.
He wanted to see green spring, not Poland.
Yet he was to meditate all his life

On Old Poland's dress and antique manners,
Or on religion, Polish, not Catholic,
And made of poor Or-Ot its priest.

What of Słonimski, sad and noble-minded?
Who thought the time of reason was at hand,
Giving himself to the future, proclaiming it
In the manner of Wells, or some other manner.
When the sky of Reason had grown bloodred,
He gave his waning years to Aeschylus,
Promised grandchildren the sight of Prometheus
Coming down a mountain in the Caucasus.

Iwaszkiewicz built his house of brilliant stones,
Indifferent to the call of public virtue.
Later on, an orator and citizen
Under the pressure of harsh necessity.
To recognize that everything is relative—
For a simple reason, because it passes—
He praised Slavic virtues to the folk,
Accompanied by a lively peasant band.
It was, all in all, a melancholy fate.

Not morally superior, just more proud,
That solitude among American winters.
The trace of a bird in snow, as always.

Time doesn't hurt anymore, nor help much.
A blue jay, kin to the Carpathian one,
Would peer into Wierzyński's window.
Oh, in the end there is a price exacted
For a young man's joy, for spring and wine.

There had never been such a Pléiade!
Yet something in their speech was flawed,
A flaw of harmony, as in their masters.
The transformed choir did not much resemble
The disorderly choir of ordinary things.

It was there everything sprouted, fermented,
Deeper than a rounded word can reach.
Tuwim lived in awe, twisted his fingers,
His face broke out in reddish, hectic spots.
One could say that he fooled the officials,
Just as he later cheated earnest Communists.
It choked him. Inside his scream was another:
That human life was chaos and a marvel,
That we walk, eat, talk, and at the same time
The light of eternity shines on our souls.

There are those who see a pretty, smiling girl
And imagine a skeleton with rings on the bones.
Such was Tuwim. He aspired to long poems.

But his thought was conventional, used
As easily as he used assonance and rhyme,
To cover his visions, of which he grew ashamed.

Whoever, in this century, forms letters
In ordered lines on a sheet of paper
Hears knockings, the voices of poor spirits
Imprisoned in a table, a wall, a vase
Of flowers. They seem to want to remind us
Whose hands brought all these objects into being.
Hours of labor, boredom, hopelessness
Live inside things and will not disappear.
The one who holds the pen, to whom this world
Of things is given, feels uneasy, is afraid.
He tries to achieve a childish innocence,
But the magic had fled from magic spells.

That's why it was that the new generation
Liked these poets only moderately,
Paid them tribute, but with a certain anger.
It wanted to stutter programmatically,
For a stutterer at least expressed a sense.
Nor did Broniewski win their admiration,
Though he took something strong from underground
Worked up as stanzas for the working class.
The Spring of Nations, for the second time,
Turned out to be melodious bel canto.

What they really wanted was a new Whitman
Who, amidst the wagoners and lumbermen,
Would make everyday life shine out like the sun.
Who would see in tongs, hammers, planes and chisels
Brilliant man running through the cosmos.

In the swarm of the Kraków avant-garde
Only Przyboś merits our surprise.
Nations and countries crumbled to dust,
To ashes, and Przyboś remained Przyboś.
No madness ate at his heart, which is human,
And thus intelligible. What was his secret?
In Shakespeare's time they called it euphuism.
A style composed of metaphor entirely.
Przyboś was a rationalist deep down.
He felt what a reasonable social person
Was supposed to feel, thought what they thought.
He wanted to put motion into static images.

And the avant-garde made the usual mistake.
They renovated an old Krakóvian rite:
Ascribing to language more importance
Than it could, without ridicule, sustain.
They must have known that from clenched jaws
Their voice issued in a strange falsetto
And that their dream of a folkish strength
Was the subterfuge of a frightened art.

Let us reach deeper. This was a time of schism.
"God and country" had ceased to be a lure.
A poet despised a cavalry officer more
Than bohemians had once despised a banker.
He mocked national banners and a show of flag,
Would spit when a crowd of screaming youths
Marched, wielding canes, against a Jewish merchant.

The end was prepared in advance. It was not
For lack of armor and cannon that the Republic fell.
In Poland a poet is a barometer,
Even if he published in *Linia* or *Kwadryga*.
A skein of common values came undone.
No common faith bound our minds together.
Those who saw took refuge in irony
And lived in the crowd as on a desert island.
One of those who understood pretended
To worship the gods the nation worshipped.

Gałczyński wanted to fall on his knees.
His story contains an elemental truth,
Namely, that a poet without community
Rustles in the wind like dry grass in December.
It's not up to him to put custom in doubt
Unless he's ready to be ostracized.
Let it be stated here clearly: the Party

Descends directly from the fascist Right.
Outside of them there was never anything
But rebels whose posturing merited scorn.
Who resurrected the sword of Bolesław the Brave?
Who drove pillars into the bottom of the Oder?
And who recognized that the way to power
Was to blow on the coals of national passions?

Gałczyński tied these elements together:
Jeering at the middle class, evoking Scythian
Virtues, penning a Polish Horst Wessel lied.
His fame has burgeoned through two epochs.

Czechowicz, the bucolic, was quite different.
Thatched huts, a patch of cumin and carrots,
A clear, lustrous morning by the river,
Which carries the echo of a Kuyavian dance
Sung by women washing linen in a stream.
He loved everything small. He made the idyll
Of a land with no politics and no defenses.
Be good to him, you birds and trees. Guard him,
From ravaging time protect his grave in Lublin.

Not one nation but a hundred nations
Appealed to Szenwald. And though a Stalinist
He knew how to profit from Marx and the Greeks.

A scene by a brook: a school excursion encounters
Barefoot peasant children stealing wood for fuel.
Or the tale of a little worker's child for whom
A bicycle is miracle and inspiration.
Poetry has nothing to do with morals,
As Szenwald, a Red Army lieutenant, proved.
At a time when, in the gulags of the north,
The corpses of a hundred nations whitened,
He was writing an ode to Mother Siberia,
One of the finer Polish-language poems.

On a steep street somewhere a schoolboy
Comes home from the library, carrying a book.
The book has a title: *Afloat in the Forest*.
Stained by the fingers of diligent Indians.
A ray of sunlight on Amazon lianas,
Leaves spreading on the green water in mats
So thick a man can walk across them.
The dreamer wanders from one bank to the other,
The monkeys, brown and hairy as a nut,
Make hanging bridges in trees above his head.

He is the future reader of our poets.
Impervious to crooked fences, the calling of crows
In cloudy skies, he lives among his marvels,
And, if he survives destruction, it is he

Who will preserve with tenderness his guides,
Iwaszkiewicz, Lechoń, and Słonimski.
Wierzyński and Tuwim will live forever
As they lived in his young and ardent mind.
He won't ask who is greater, who is less,
Finding in each of them a different nuance,
While a pirogue takes him up some Amazon.

For him Wittlin puts a spoonful of soup
Into the grizzled mouth of human hunger,
Baliński hears bells of a meandering caravan
In the rosy gray dusks of dusty Isfahan.
Ważyk eyes the ship model in a window
And a wave sparkles in the poems of Apollinaire.
And there was, to be heard, the exquisite lament
of a Polish Sappho, Ursula's, renewed
After four hundred years. Life fades quickly
And the turning disk preserves, longer even
Than the velvet of Caruso, that complaint
Of Maria Pawlikowska: "*Perchè? Perchè?*"
Perhaps it was not for nothing, the soldier's blood
Darkening into small stars beneath a birch.
Piłsudski should not shoulder all the blame—
Though he cared only for a secure border.
He bought us twenty years, he wore a cloak
Of injury and guilt, so that beauty

Had a little space to grow, though beauty is,
It's often said, a matter of no importance.

Young reader, you won't live inside a rose.
That country has its planets, its rivers,
But it is as frail as the edge of the morning.
It's we who create it every day anew,
By respecting as real many more things
Than are frozen between a noun and its sound.
We wrest them into the world by force.
If got too easily, they don't exist at all.
So, farewell, things gone. Your echo calls us,
But we need to speak gracelessly and roughly.

The last poem of the epoch went to print.
Its author, Władysław Sebyła,
Liked to take his violin from the wardrobe,
Putting its case by the volumes of Norwid.
He kept the collar of his blue uniform
Unbuttoned (He worked for the railway at Praga).
In that poem, as if it were his last will,
Poland is the ancient, two-faced god
Swiatowid, listening as the drums beat closer
On plains to the east, plains to the west,
While in its sleep the country dreams of bees
Buzzing through noons in Hesperidian groves.

Was it for this they shot him in the head
And buried his body in a Smolensk forest?

A beautiful night. A huge, lambent moon
Pours down a light that only happens
In September. In the hours before dawn
The air above Warsaw is utterly silent.
Barrage balloons hang like ripened fruit
In a sky just grown silvery with dawn.

On Tamka Street a girl's heels click.
She calls in a half whisper. They go together
To an empty lot overgrown with weeds.
A watchman on duty, hidden in the shadows,
Hears their soft voices in the bedding dark.
I do not know how to bear my pity.

Or how to find words for our common plight.
A little whore and a worker from Tamka.
Before them, the terror of the rising sun.
Later I would ask myself more than once
What became of them in the coming years and ages.

PART THREE

THE SPIRIT OF HISTORY

Warsaw, 1939–1945

III. THE SPIRIT OF HISTORY

When gold paint flakes from the arms of sculptures,
When the letter falls out of the book of laws,
Then consciousness is naked as an eye.

When the pages of books fall in fiery scraps
Onto smashed leaves and twisted metal,
The tree of good and evil is stripped bare.

When a wing made of canvas is extinguished
In a potato patch, when steel disintegrates,
Nothing is left but straw huts and cow dung.

In Masovian forest, on needle-covered paths,
Between the Reich and the General Government,
The flat feet of a peasant woman in the sand.
She stops, backs her burden against a pine
And pulls a thorn from her dust-covered foot.
A slab of butter in a wet rag is molded
To the shape of her archaic shoulder bones.
There's a shuffle for places at the ferry.

Chickens cackle. Geese stretch their necks from baskets.
In the town, a bullet is carving a dry trace
In the sidewalk near bags of homegrown tobacco.

All night long, on the outskirts of the city,
An old Jew, tossed in a clay pit, has been dying.
His moans subside only when the sun comes up.
The Vistula is gray, it washes through osiers
And fashions fans of gravel in the shallows.
An overburdened steamer, with its smugglers' load,
Churns up white froth with its paddle wheel.
Stanisław, or Henryk, sounds the bottom with a pole.
"Meter." Chlup. "Meter." Chlup. "Meter Twenty."

Where wind carries the smell of the crematorium
And a bell in the village tolls the Angelus,
The Spirit of History is out walking.
He whistles, he likes these countries washed
By a deluge, deprived of shape and now ready.
A worm-fence, a homespun skirt is pleasant to him,
The same in Poland, in India, Arabia.

He stretches his thick fingers toward the sky.
Under his palm, a rider on a bicycle:
The organizer of a security network,
A delegate of the military faction in London.
Poplars, as tiny as rye plants in a gully,
Conduct the eye to the roof of a manor
From the forest, and there, in the dining room,
Tired boys are lounging in officers' boots.

A poet has already recognized the walker,
An inferior god to whom time and the fate
Of one-day-long kingdoms is submitted.
His face is the size of ten moons. He wears
About his neck a chain of severed heads.
Who does not acknowledge him begins to mumble.
Whoever bows to him attracts his scorn.

Lutes, arcadian groves, and leaves of laurel,
Bright ladies, princes with consorts, where are you?
You could be courted with a well-turned phrase,
A graceful leap to catch a bag of gold.
He asks for more. He asks for flesh and blood.

Who are you, Powerful One? The nights are long.
Do we know you as the Spirit of the Earth,
Shaking down caterpillars from an apple tree
So that the thrushes have an easy gleaning?
Who gathers beetles' legs for a fecund humus
From which in time the hyacinth flowers?

Are you and he the same, O Destroyer?
He, inseparable, our faithful companion,
How many times has he guided our hand
Along the shoulder and neck of a girl,
When couples walked in the dusks of July

Through a meadow, in the scent of pines,
While a harmonium plays a melody, unreal,
About lemon trees and an island of lovers
So utterly lost it is painful to think of?
How many times has he, beauty and glory,
Splendor and the mating cries of grouse,
Curled our lips into an ironic smile
By whispering in our ears that spring,
the nightingale's trill, our own inspiration,
Are his prodigal lures, so that the law
Of the species is fulfilled. It will cool,
our blood, and we, touched by rust, dressed
In our cloaks of fading purple, will fall
Down into the dust of a million years, mingled
At last with our cousin pithecanthropus
Who's been waiting. And you, is it just that you,
in a reasonable frock like Hegel's,
Have chosen for yourself a different name?

Clandestine bulletins in a green bag.
The poet who reads them hears him laughing.
"For punishment I took away their reason.
No one will think to step outside my will."

With what word to reach into the future,
With what word to defend human happiness—

It has the smell of freshly baked bread—
If the language of poets cannot search out
Standards of use to later generations?
We have not been taught. We do not know at all
How to unite Freedom and Necessity.

In a dream the mind visits two sharp edges.
Woe to the unearthly, the radiant ones.
While storming heaven, they neglect the Earth
With its joy and warmth and animal strength.
Woe to the reasonable, the heavy-minded.
Their lies will extinguish the morning star,
A gift more durable than Nature is, or Death.

Clandestine bulletins in a green bag.
The poem of propaganda will not last.
It's false because it knows less than we know.
Poetry feels too much. Therefore its silence.
Still it responds to a distant call,
Not ready to bear the weight of something new.

The twenty-year-old poets of Warsaw
Did not want to know that something in this century
Submits to thought, not to Davids with their slings.
They were like a man in a hospital room
Who, indifferent to pacts with the future,

Wants to be faithful only to the moment,
Wants to possess the laughter of children,
The aerial games of the birds, at least once,
For the last time, before the stone gate closes.
The makeshift barricade was not adorned
With mankind's auroras, bards' promises.
Over a yellow field and a ring of the dead
In combat, Madonna stood, wounded by a sword.

The young, amazed by every morning, touched
A table or a chair, as if they had found
An entire puffball gleaming in the rain,
Intact. Objects for them were rainbows,
Misty as their years sent out before them.
They had to let go of fame, peace, wisdom.
Their poems were a prayer for manfulness
"When they chase us from life as from a city,
Oh you, our golden home, secure us a bed
Of malachite, only for the night, though it's eternal."
No ancient Greek hero entered into combat
So deprived of hope, in their heads the image
Of a white skull kicked by feet in passing.

Copernicus: the statue of a German or a Pole?
Leaving a spray of flowers, Bojarski perished:
A sacrifice should be pure, unreasoned.

Trzebiński, the new Polish Nietzsche,
Had his mouth plastered shut before he died.
He took with him the view of a wall, low clouds
His black eyes had just a moment to absorb.
Baczyński's head fell against his rifle.
The uprising scared up flocks of pigeons.
Gajcy, Stroiński were raised to the sky,
A red sky, on the shield of an explosion.

Under a linden tree, as before, daylight
Quivered on a goose quill dipped in ink.
Books were still governed by the old rule,
Born of a belief that visible beauty
Is a little mirror for the beauty of being.
The survivors ran through fields, escaping
From themselves, knowing they wouldn't return
For a hundred years. Before them were spread
Those quicksands where a tree changes into nothing,
Into an anti-tree, where no borderline
Separates a shape from a shape, and where,
Amid thunder, the golden house of *is*
Collapses, and the word *becoming* ascends.

Till the end of their days all of them
Carried the memory of their cowardice,
For they didn't want to die without a reason.

Now He, expected, for a long time awaited,
Raised up the smoke of a thousand censers.
They crawled on slippery paths to his feet.

—"King of the centuries, ungraspable Movement,
You who fill the grottoes of the ocean
With a roiling silence, who dwell in the blood
Of the gored shark devoured by other sharks,
In the whistle of a half-bird, half-fish,
In the thundering sea, in the iron gurgling
Of the rocks when archipelagoes surge up.

"The churning of your surf casts up bracelets,
Pearls not eyes, bones from which the salt
Has eaten crowns and dresses of brocade.
You without beginning, you always between
A form and a form, O stream, bright spark,
Antithesis that ripens toward a thesis,
Now we have become equal to the gods,
Knowing, in you, that we do not exist.

"You, in whom cause is married to effect,
Drew us from the depth as you draw a wave,
For one instant, limitless, of transformation.
You have shown us the agony of this age
So that we could ascend to those heights
Where your hand commands the instruments.

Spare us, do not punish us. Our offense
Was grave: we forgot the power of your law.
Save us from ignorance. Accept now our devotion."

So they forswore. But every one of them
Kept hidden a hope that the possessions of time
Were assigned a limit. That they would one day
Be able to look at a cherry tree in blossom,
For a moment, unique among the moments,
Put the ocean to sleep, close the hourglass,
And listen to how the clocks stop ticking.

When they put a rope around my neck,
When they choke off my breath with a rope,
I'll turn around once, and what will I be?

When they give me an injection of phenol,
When I walk half a step with phenol in my veins,
What wisdom of the prophets will enlighten me?

When they tear us from this one embrace,
When they destroy forever the shaft of tender light,
What Heaven will see us reunited?

A singer cursed white clouds above the ghetto.
I used to give pennies to the blind poet.
Let his songs stay with me to the end.

On the wall of my cell for a whole night I carved
A word of love, so that syllables survive,
And roll with this prison around the sun.

I was beating the rhythm on an empty can,
I who am not, who only was once,
There where the road led to the camp gate.

My trace, a diary hidden between bricks.
Perhaps someday it will be unearthed,
A day of forgiveness or a day of penance.

Soil of annihilation, soil of hate,
No word will purify it ever.
No such poet will be born.

For even if one had been called, he walked
Beside us to the last gate, for only
A child of the ghetto could utter the words.

The awkward speech of Slavic peasants
Was busy for centuries with rustling rhymes:
It produced at last an anonymous song
Still audible in the trembling of the air,
There where white foam hisses under palm trees
And where an osprey in the Labrador currents

Plunges to the sea, a plough of brightness
Beneath the firs of Maine. A madrigal
Humming on the strings of a viola, simple,
A song for ladies in a pretty season
Whose meaning time just happened to reverse.

Winter will end

Marching girls, Jewish,
Expressed their only joy, of vengeance.
Yes, soon at night the voice of flying cranes.
Soon the dry snow will numb no worker's hand.
Yes, in a stream a pebble as rosy as lips
Will crunch in the streambed under a passing foot.

Spring will arrive

Yes, juices will surge in the tulip
And a May beetle, humming, tap at a window.
Yes, a bridegroom will pick young leaves of the oak
To plait a wreath for his bride.

Above our bodies

Our bodies are one body now.
Bone, muscle, nerves not mine but ours.

The names of Miriam, Sonia, Rachel
Darken and cool in the slow air.

Grass will thrive.

Grass, defeated by the irony of a song.

Pickled cucumbers in a sweating jar.
A sprig of dill. Cucumbers are eternal.
Early morning twigs crackle on the hearth.
In a clay bowl wooden spoons and gruel.
At the door baskets and hoes where hens roost.
And the dead-straight farm track, fields without limit.
Plains, empty and misty, to Skierniewice.
Plains, empty and misty, to the Ural Mountains.
Hey, don't rest yet. Noon is a long way off.

Light Nanking silk our shoulders adorn,
In a circle of well-born youth we sit.
We pass in dressing the hours of the morn
And evenings we sharpen our wit.

Above potato fields and the autumn earth,
A spark like a snowflake: an aeroplane
Rolling and turning, high up, beyond the clouds.

Say what you desire
Tell us your hungers and your thirsts.

No need for the bitterness of mustard seed.
Poetry is well served by warm porcelains,
By the company of a clutch of charming Graces,
By essences distilled from classical herbs.
Puffing his pipe, dressed in Nanking fabric,
Let the poet pursue his wayward dreams.
A wooden house, of course, but well-made, plumb.

The *Phaedo* at arm's length, also Cato's *Life*.
On Friday evenings the family would light
A row of candles in bright chandeliers.
From the rhythms of Daniel, rhythms of Isaiah,
A young man received more than enough instruction
In how to keep silent, how to compose a verse.

A castle sits on the Nowogródek hill.

What we do need are forests, clear waters.
For there's nothing here to defend a man.
When he studies the void of the horizon
The idea of a center slowly fades.
His only counsel is his moving shadow.

The man not born to these level plains
Will sail the seas, wander the country
On the banks of the Vezere under apple trees
Or chase the reflection of his homeland
In the pines and black-green rivers of Maine
As one scans the faces in a crowd of strangers
For that one face, uniquely and ardently loved.

Mickiewicz is too difficult for us.
Ours is not a lordly or a Jewish knowledge.
We worked with a plough, with a harrow.
On feast days we heard another music.

Ho la ho la
Lambs bleat baa baa
Shepherds run to see
Come to the stable
As soon as you're able
Ho la ho la
Even Jack with his stutter
Sings to the Mother
The Holy Mother
Ho la

The double bass with its huge belly buzzes.

Hu du hu du
We are playing too

We sing to Christ the Lord
Not for a reward
Hu du

The violin, made from linden, thinly wails.

Ti ri ti ri
We play a joyous trill
Wa li wa li
From dawn to evening still
Wa li

Old Gregor blows and squeezes on the pipe:

Me-e lee me-e lay
To the child we play

And the clarinet is not far behind:

mu-la mu-la
To the mother and the child

And the double bass repeats:

Hu du hu du
We are playing too
We play for Christ the Lord

So many things have passed, so many things.
And while no work accomplished helps us,
Tytus Czyzewski returns with his Christmas carol.
The double bass used to boom, so he booms.

I rolled a cigarette and licked the paper.
Then a match in the little house of my hand.
And why not a tinderbox with flint?
The wind was blowing. I sat on the road at noon,
Thinking and thinking. Beside me, potatoes.

PART FOUR

Natura

Pennsylvania, 1948–1949

IV. NATURA

The garden of Nature opens.
The grass at the threshold is green.
And an almond tree begins to bloom.

Sunt mihi Dei Acherontis propitii!
Valeat numen triplex Jehovae!
Ignis, aeris, aquae, terrae spiritus,
Salvete!—says the entering guest.

Ariel lives in the palace of an apple tree,
But will not appear, vibrating like a wasp's wing,
And Mephistopheles, disguised as an abbot
Of the Dominicans or the Franciscans,
Will not descend from a mulberry bush
Onto a pentagram drawn in the black loam of the path.

But a rhododendron walks among the rocks
Shod in leathery leaves and ringing a pink bell.
A hummingbird, a child's top in the air,
Hovers in one spot, the beating heart of motion.
Impaled on the nail of a black thorn, a grasshopper
Leaks brown fluid from its twitching snout.
And what can he do, the phantom-in-chief,

As he's been called, more than a magician,
The *Socrates of snails*, as he's been called,
Musician of pears, arbiter of orioles, man?
In sculptures and canvases our individuality
Manages to survive. In Nature it perishes.
Let him accompany the coffin of the woodsman
Pushed from a cliff by a mountain demon,
The he-goat with its jutting curl of horn.
Let him visit the graveyard of the whalers
Who drove spears into the flesh of leviathan
And looked for the secret in guts and blubber.
The thrashing subsided, quieted to waves.
Let him unroll the textbooks of alchemists
Who almost found the cipher, thus the scepter.
Then passed away without hands, eyes, or elixir.

Here there is sun. And whoever, as a child,
Believed he could break the repeatable pattern
Of things, if only he understood the pattern,
Is cast down, rots in the skin of others,
Looks with wonder at the colors of the butterfly,
Inexpressible wonder, formless, hostile to art.

To keep the oars from squeaking in their locks,
He binds them with a handkerchief. The dark
Had rushed east from the Rocky Mountains
And settled in the forests of the continent:

Sky full of embers reflected in a cloud,
Flights of herons, trees above a marsh,
The dry stalks in water, livid, black. My boat
Divides the aerial utopias of the mosquitoes
Which rebuild their glowing castles instantly.
A water lily sinks, fizzing, under the boat's bow.

Now it is night only. The water is ash-gray.
Play, music, but inaudibly! I wait an hour
In the silence, senses tuned to a beaver's lodge.
Then suddenly, a crease in the water, a beast's
black moon, rounded, ploughing up quickly
from the pond-dark, from the bubbling methanes.
I am not immaterial and never will be.
My scent in the air, my animal smell,
Spreads, rainbow-like, scares the beaver:
A sudden *splat*.
                              I remained where I was
In the high, soft coffer of the night's velvet,
Mastering what had come to my senses:
How the four-toed paws worked, how the hair
Shook off water in the muddy tunnel.
It does not know time, hasn't heard of death,
Is submitted to me because I know I'll die.

I remember everything. That wedding in Basel,
A touch to the strings of a viola and fruit

In silver bowls. As was the custom in Savoy,
An overturned cup for three pair of lips,
And the wine spilled. The flames of the candles
Wavery and frail in a breeze from the Rhine.
Her fingers, bones shining through the skin,
Felt out the hooks and clasps of the silk
And the dress opened like a nutshell,
Fell from the turned graininess of the belly.
A chain for the neck rustled without epoch,
In pits where the arms of various creeds
Mingle with bird cries and the red hair of caesars.

Perhaps this is only my own love speaking
Beyond the seventh river. Grit of subjectivity,
Obsession, bar the way to it.
Until a window shutter, dogs in the cold garden,
The whistle of a train, an owl in the firs
Are spared the distortions of memory.
And the grass says: how it was I don't know.

Splash of a beaver in the American night.
The memory grows larger than my life.
A tin plate, dropped on the irregular red bricks
Of a floor, rattles tinnily forever.
Belinda of the big foot, Julia, Thaïs,
The tufts of their sex shadowed by ribbon.

Peace to the princesses under the tamarisks.
Desert winds beat against their painted eyelids.
Before the body was wrapped in bandelettes,
Before wheat fell asleep in the tomb,
Before stone fell silent, and there was only pity.

Yesterday a snake crossed the road at dusk.
Crushed by a tire, it writhed on the asphalt.
We are both the snake and the wheel.
There are two dimensions. Here is the unattainable
Truth of being, here, at the edge of lasting
and not lasting. Where the parallel lines intersect,
Time lifted above time by time.

Before the butterfly and its color, he, numb,
Formless, feels his fear, he, unattainable.
For what is a butterfly without Julia and Thaïs?
And what is Julia without a butterfly's down
In her eyes, her hair, the smooth grain of her belly?
The kingdom, you say. We do not belong to it,
And still, in the same instant, we belong.
For how long will a nonsensical Poland
Where poets write of their emotions as if
They had a contract of limited liability
Suffice? I want not poetry, but a new diction,
Because only it might allow us to express

A new tenderness and save us from a law
That is not our law, from necessity
Which is not ours, even if we take its name.

From broken armor, from eyes stricken
By the command of time and taken back
Into the jurisdiction of mold and fermentation,
We draw our hope. Yes, to gather in an image
The furriness of the beaver, the smell of rushes,
And the wrinkles of a hand holding a pitcher
From which wine trickles. Why cry out
That a sense of history destroys our substance
If it, precisely, is offered to our powers,
A muse of our gray-haired father, Herodotus,
As our arm and our instrument, though
It is not easy to use it, to strengthen it
So that, like a plumb with a pure gold center,
It will serve again to rescue human beings.

With such reflections I pushed a rowboat,
In the middle of the continent, through tangled stalks,
In my mind an image of the waves of two oceans
And the slow rocking of a guard-ship's lantern.
Aware that at this moment I—and not only I—
Keep, as in a seed, the unnamed future.
And then a rhythmic appeal composed itself,
Alien to the moth with its whirring of silk:

O City, O Society, O Capital,
We have seen your steaming entrails.
You will no longer be what you have been.
Your songs no longer gratify our hearts.

Steel, cement, lime, law, ordinance,
We have worshipped you too long,
You were for us a goal and a defense,
Ours was your glory and your shame.

And where was the covenant broken?
Was it in the fires of war, the incandescent sky?
Or at twilight, as the towers fly past, when one looked
From the train across a desert of tracks

To a window out past the maneuvering locomotives
Where a girl examines her narrow, moody face
In a mirror and ties a ribbon to her hair
Pierced by the sparks of curling papers?

Those walls of yours are shadows of walls,
And your light disappeared forever.
Not the world's monument anymore, an oeuvre of our own
Stands beneath the sun in an altered space.

From stucco and mirrors, glass and paintings,
Tearing aside curtains of silver and cotton,

Comes man, naked and mortal,
Ready for truth, for speech, for wings.

Lament, Republic! Fall to your knees!
The loudspeaker's spell is discontinued.
Listen! You can hear the clocks ticking.
Your death approaches by his hand.

An oar over my shoulder, I walked from the woods.
A porcupine scolded from the fork of a tree,
A horned owl, not changed by the century,
Not changed by place or time, looked down.
Bubo maximus, from the work of Linnaeus.

America for me has the pelt of a raccoon,
Its eyes are a raccoon's black binoculars.
A chipmunk flickers in a litter of dry bark
Where ivy and vines tangle in the red soil
At the roots of an arcade of tulip trees.
America's wings are the color of a cardinal,
Its beak is half-open and a mockingbird trills
From a leafy bush in the sweat-bath of the air.
Its line is the wavy body of a water moccasin
Crossing a river with a grass-like motion,
A rattlesnake, a rubble of dots and speckles,
Coiling under the bloom of a yucca plant.

America is for me the illustrated version
Of childhood tales about the heart of tanglewood,
Told in the evening to the spinning wheel's hum.
And a violin, shivvying up a square dance,
Plays the fiddles of Lithuania or Flanders.
My dancing partner's name is Birute Swenson.
She married a Swede, but was born in Kaunas.
Then from the night window a moth flies in
As big as the joined palms of the hands,
With a hue like the transparency of emeralds.

Why not establish a home in the neon heat
of Nature? Is it not enough, the labor of autumn,
Of winter and spring and withering summer?
You will hear not one word spoken of the court
of Sigismund Augustus on the banks of the Delaware River.
The Dismissal of the Greek Envoys is not needed.
Herodotus will repose on his shelf, uncut.
And the rose only, a sexual symbol,
Symbol of love and superterrestrial beauty,
Will open a chasm deeper than your knowledge.
About it we find a song in a dream:

Inside the rose
Are houses of gold,
black isobars, streams of cold.

Dawn touches her finger to the edge of the Alps
And evening streams down to the bays of the sea.

If anyone dies inside the rose,
They carry him down the purple-red road
In a procession of clocks all wrapped in folds.
They light up the petals of grottoes with torches.
They bury him there where color begins,
At the source of the sighing,
Inside the rose.

Let names of months mean only what they mean.
Let the *Aurora*'s cannons be heard in none
Of them, or the tread of young rebels marching.
We might, at best, keep some kind of souvenir,
Preserved like a fan in a garret. Why not
Sit down at a rough country table and compose
An ode in the old manner, as in the old times
Chasing a beetle with the nib of our pen?

ODE

O October
You are my true delight,
Month of the cranberry and the red of the maple,
Of Hudson Bay geese a-wing in the transparent air,
Dry vines and withering grasses and smoky light,
Oh October

O October
The silence of roads in a carpet of pine needles,
A birdcall fashioned from an owl's wing,
The wailing of dogs on the scent of a buck,
And the startled peal of a bird in the spruces,
Oh October

O October
Shine of frost on the blade of a sword
When a Polish engineer glimpses near West Point
In the vivid woods the maple-red coats of British soldiers
Moving soundlessly up the Appalachian trail,
Oh October

O October
Cold is your crystal wine,
Tart is the taste of your lips above a necklace of rowanberries,

Your panting sides are the color
Of the fallow hair of a mountain deer,
Oh October

O October
Pouring dew on the rusty traces,
Blowing a bufflo horn above the rebel camp,
Burning bare feet on the sloping hill paths
When the smokes of autumn and of cannons drift past,
Oh October

O October
Season of poetry, of the total daring
Of starting one's life at every moment anew,
You gave me the magic ring which, when turned,
Sends down a gleam from your jewel of freedom,
Oh October

There is much with which to reproach us.
Given the choice, we rejected peaceful silence
And long meditation on the structure of the world
Which deserves respect. Neither the eternal moment
Attracted us as it should, nor purity of style.
We wanted, instead, to move as words move,
Raising the dust of names and of events.
We didn't care enough that they disappear
In a thousand sparks and we with them. Even

The disrepute we have taken on ourselves
Was not completely far from our designs,
And so, though unwillingly, we pay the price.

Many a man will concede, if he knows himself,
That he was like one who hears a chorus
Of voices and doesn't know what they mean.
Thence, fury. A foot to the accelerator, as if
Speed could save us from voices and phantoms.
We trailed everywhere an invisible rope
And felt its hook inside us every moment.

And yet the accusers were mistaken, if,
Shedding tears over the evils of this age,
They saw us as angels, hurled into an abyss,
Shaking our fists at the works of God.
There is no doubt that many perished, infamously,
Because, like an illiterate discovering chemistry,
They suddenly discovered relativity and time.
For others the very roundness of a stone
Picked up on the bank of a river provided
The lesson. Or the bleeding gills of a perch,
Or—the moon rising over banks of clouds—
A beaver ploughing the slumbering softness of water.

For contemplation fades without resistance.
For its own sake, it should be forbidden.

And we, certainly, were happier than those
Who drank sadness from the books of Schopenhauer,
While they listened from their garrets to the din
Of music from the tavern down below.
At least poetry, philosophy, action were not,
For us, separated, as they were for them,
But joined in one will: we needed to be of use.
And that is the—sometimes burdensome—recompense.

If we, though our faults were merely historical,
Will not receive the laurel of long fame,
So what, after all? Some are given monuments
And mausoleums, yet in a soft May rain,
Covered by a single overcoat, a boy and girl
Rush by, entirely indifferent to that perfection.
And some word of us may remain in any case,
Some remembrance of our half-opened lips:
They did not have time to say what they wanted.

Spirits of the air, of fire, of water,
Keep close to us, but not too close.
The ship's propeller drives us from you.
It's not fullfilled: the old hope that Neptune
Will show his beard, trailing a retinue of nymphs.
Nothing but ocean which boils and repeats:
In vain, in vain. Nothingness is so strong
We try to master it by thinking of the bones

Of pirates, the silky eyebrows of governors
On which the crabs feast. And our hands grip
Harder at the cool metal of the railing.
Look for help in the smell of paint and soap.
The ship's body, creaking, carries the freight
of our foolishness, vagueness, and hidden faith,
The dirt of our subjectivity, and the homeless
White faces of the ones who were killed in combat.
Carries it where? To the isles of bliss? No,
In us storm winds drowned that stanza of Horace
A penknife worked into a wooden bench at school.
It will not find us in this salt and void:

Iam Cytherea choros ducit Venus imminente luna

BRIE-COMTE-ROBERT, 1956

AUTHOR'S NOTES

The title is ironic. The term "La Belle Epoque" was used in France to designate the beginning of the twentieth century, specifically the years preceding the outbreak of the First World War in 1914. Compared to what happened after that date, the epoch was "belle." Otherwise it hardly deserves the name.

5   *Cabbies were dozing by St. Mary's tower*: The year is roughly 1900, and we are in the medieval city of Kraków, once the capital of the kingdom of Poland, now a provincial city belonging to the Hapsburg Empire. Still, Kraków preserves vestiges of its past; it is considered the spiritual capital of Poland, a country partitioned by Russia, Prussia, and Austria in the late eighteenth century. It is also the seat of the Jagiellonian University, founded in 1364 and a center for theater and publishing. St. Mary's Church dates from the city's most prosperous era: its construction, in the Gothic

style, took some hundred years, from the middle of the fourteenth to the middle of the fifteenth century.

5   *Kraków was tiny as a painted egg*: As was usual in the Middle Ages, the city was enclosed by walls and therefore could not expand. In the nineteenth century the walls were taken down, but in 1900 urban sprawl was still in the future.

5   *In their black capes poets strolled the streets*: A black cape, a wide-brimmed hat, and a large tie called a *lavallière* were a uniform for the bohemian poets of the time.

5   *An* Ober *brings the paper on a stick*: The *café* was an institution in all the cities and towns of the Hapsburg Empire. Of course, all the vanguard movements in poetry and painting got discussed in the cafés. Sometimes a café would house a literary cabaret, as was the case with *Jama Michalikowa*— Michalik's Hole—in Kraków, seat of the "Green Balloon." The café was also the place where one read newspapers. They were attached to sticks. An *Ober*, short for *Oberkellner*, or headwaiter, was likely to bring them.

5   *Muses, Rachels in trailing shawls*: Rachel is a character in a play in verse, *The Wedding*, by Stanisław Wyspiański (1869–1907). The play was performed in 1901, became a sensation in the city and an event in the history of Polish theater. European theater had at that time moved on from its traditional habits, including stardom and realistic set design. Symbolism entered theatrical plays as well as poetry, and a unity

of mood, rhythm, and color was required by theatrical reformers. Wyspiański's ideas, in this respect, paralleled those of the English dramaturge Gordon Craig.

On a realistic level, *The Wedding* presents one night of dancing and carousing to celebrate the marriage of Wyspiański's friend, the poet Lucien Rydel, to a peasant girl from a village near Kraków. Dance music is heard throughout, and dancing couples are seen through a door to a larger room, while in the foreground, from time to time, guests appear, in pairs, to engage in dialogue. The technique derived from Christmas puppet shows, popular in Poland. The two characters corresponded to the two hands of the puppeteer.

On a symbolic level, *The Wedding* deals with the thoughts and aspirations of Polish society, a cross section of which is personified by guests from various social strata: peasants, aristocrats, merchants, the intelligentsia. Rachel, the daughter of a Jewish innkeeper, is an intellectual, a bluestocking, an admirer of poets, and that is why I call her their Muse. The action of the play is, in fact, its changing mood, which becomes more weird as the night moves toward dawn. There is the expectation, more and more intense, of an extraordinary event about to occur. Reality disintegrates into dream when Rachel invites in from the garden a straw man, a rosebush covered with straw, to join the company. The tension draws to a breaking point and collapses. At the end the straw man plays a monotonous tune on his fiddle and the assembled cast performs a dance of phantoms.

For Polish audiences the revelation so avidly expected

had a clear symbolic meaning: liberation. The partition of the country had been sanctioned by the Congress of Vienna in 1815. In other words, the extraordinary event would mean the restoration of an independent Poland— through war? uprising? revolution? Thus Polish theater served nationalist purposes, as William Butler Yeats's theater did in Ireland. Wyspiański and Yeats, who was born in 1865, were contemporaries.

5   *The pin lies with their daughters' ashes now*: The image alludes to the Holocaust. Rachel herself, had she lived into the 1940s, would have perished at the hands of the Nazis, as her daughters would have. The objects enumerated, a pin, seashells, a glass lily, could have been found in any of the apartments of the middle class in that epoch, as a tribute to the rule of fashion.

5   *Angels of Art Nouveau*: In Polish, I call them "Angels of Secession." At the end of the nineteenth century a new style in art was proclaimed by groups of European painters. In Vienna such a group seceded from an official exhibition in 1897 and had an exhibition of their own, hence the name used in Vienna and Kraków and Prague to designate the style also called Art Nouveau.

5   *In the dark WC's of their parents' homes, / Meditating on the link between sex and the soul*: A mastermind of modernism in Polish literature, Stanisław Przybyszewski (1868–1927) an-

nounced in a magazine he edited in Kraków: "In the beginning was Lust." This peculiar transformation of the opening of the gospel of John corresponded to new trends in philosophy and psychiatry. Przybyszewski had studied psychiatry in Berlin: thus it was not necessary to wait for Freud, who made his way to fame at more or less the same time.

5 *(Dr. Freud, I hear, is also from Galicia)*: Sigmund Freud was born in Moravia, but his ancestors presumably lived in the neighboring province of Galicia, the northern district of the Hapsburg Empire which contained the cities of Kraków and Lvov.

5 *And Anna Csilag grew her long, long hair*: All the newspapers of the Hapsburg Empire used to reproduce a photograph of this girl from Moravia as publicity for a pharmaceutical product. She had, by applying it, grown her hair down to her feet.

5 *The hussars' tunics were trimmed out with braid*: The hussars, Hungarian cavalry detachments, were known by their elaborate uniforms.

5 *News of the emperor spread through mountain villages*: Emperor Franz Josef liked to present himself as a protector of peasants. He was very popular among them and among the inhabitants of the mountain villages south of Kraków.

5　*This is our beginning. Useless to deny it./Useless to recall a distant golden age*: "Our beginning" denotes the beginning of modern Polish poetry and of modern poetry in several other European countries. "A distant golden age" can be interpreted in two ways—as an era of harmony and happiness located in the past by Greek mythology, and as the time in the sixteenth century when old Poland and its literature flourished, when Jan Kochanowski (1530–1584) established the canon of Polish verse.

6　*Lament, Europe! And wait for a* Schiffskarte: People from the overpopulated rural areas of Europe saw their hope in migrating overseas to the industrial centers of North America. A *Schiffskarte*—a ship ticket—would enable the passage, but it had to be sent from America by relatives or by a recruiting agency.

6　*In some peasant, Slovenian or Polish, dialect*: In general, emigrants came from the villages of east-central Europe and spoke a number of Slavic idioms—Slovene, Czech, Slovak, and Polish.

6　*A pianola, hit by a bullet, begins to play*: A beloved piece of comic business in films dealing with that era.

6　*And she, fat, red-haired, snapping her garter*: It was a time of prosperous bordellos, since the still-enforced Victorian code of behavior required chastity from women before marriage. The mystery of sex was thus for men mostly personified by prostitutes. Syphilis was an affliction of that epoch, just as tuberculosis was an affliction of the first half of the nineteenth century. Among its victims were many artists and writers: Friedrich Nietzsche, Guy de Maupassant, Paul Gauguin, Stanisław Wyspiański. As a preventive measure against the disease, a product named Salvarsan was used, and, of course, condoms were peddled as a prophylactic.

6   *Max Linder leads a cow and falls down flat*: One of film's first stars was the French comic actor Max Linder, whose little comedies represented a rather primitive kind of humor. Yet the cinema undoubtedly influenced modern poetry, and therefore finds its place here.

6   *In open-air cafés lamps shine through the leaves*: Garden cafés were popular then. Women's orchestras were typical attractions. They played tunes from operettas like Lehár's *Merry Widow*. The idea of an orchestra composed of women had about it a tinge of something slightly indecent, and therefore, of course, enticing.

6   *Till from hands, jeweled rings, lilac corsets*: Women's corsets evoke in our imagination fashions from the Victorian era. By the beginning of the twentieth century, they had begun to disappear, but around 1914 they were still in use and always in the conventional lilac color.

7   *The command* "Vorwarts!" "En avant!" "Allez!": Commands
in French and German began World War I, the causes of
which remain enigmatic even today. No rational explana-
tion has been given for the wild enthusiasm of the crowds
in Berlin and Paris and Vienna at the news of the declara-
tion of war. Ahead of these people were four years of mu-
tual massacre that looked like an ordeal sent by vengeful
gods, and neither side dared to stop the slaughter.

The war put an end to the European dream of progress
and wealth, the driving force of democracy and capitalism
since the Napoleonic wars. It also put an end to the political
status quo maintained by monarchs since the Congress of
Vienna. The map of Europe was to change. The multina-
tional Hapsburg Empire disintegrated into independent
national states. Germany was to live through the moral and
economic collapse of defeat, tsarist Russia was to crumble
in the revolution. Yet perhaps the most crucial, though
rarely mentioned, aspect of the new situation was the loss
on the battlefield of a generation of gifted and energetic
potential leaders of the Europe to come, German, French,
and English. Europe as a whole lost that war and left open
the field of opportunity and competition to the United
States.

7   *The sound of a lyre from a garret window / Hums in the dawn above a*
Tingeltangel: The social status of the poet was not high. Like
other impecunious artists, he usually lived in a garret.
Tingeltangels, or dance halls, the equivalent of today's discos,
attracted a large public.

7   *A pure thing, against the sad affairs of earth*: The search for a "pure poetry," for "the essence of poetry," began in Europe toward the end of the nineteenth century. It was connected with the cultural influence of France. Stéphane Mallarmé (1842–1898) was a contemporary of the Impressionist painters. In his approach to poetry and their approach to painting, certain analogies can be found, limited, necessarily, by the fundamental difference in medium. Mallarmé and his disciples, the Symbolists, turned their backs on the public and tried to create a refined art incomprehensible to the average taste. Their ideal, and the object of their envy, was music, which was thought to convey "the ineffable," what could not be translated into human speech. Lyric poetry, according to them, had no other duty than its own perfection. In that way it was art for art's sake. This perfection was achieved through maximal condensation (i.e., the rejection of words which do not absolutely serve the composition of a given poem). The indirect effect would be, as Mallarmé said, "the purification of the language of the tribe." Another component of Symbolist aesthetics was the discovery of the work of Arthur Rimbaud (1854–1891) and the growing legend of the *poète maudit*, the damned poet, who abandoned writing to become an arms dealer in Africa. His writing, in verse and rhythmical prose, departed radically from the practice of his predecessors, though a certain continuity can be found in the writings of Charles Baudelaire (1821–1867).

The influence of these aesthetic developments was felt in various European languages, though the results differed from country to country. The translations of the Symbolists into Polish or Russian are an interesting demonstration of the ways in which every language is bound by its own laws of versification.

Besides, let us not exaggerate French influence, which favored the search for essence at the expense of range, and thus discouraged the kind of poetry that describes everyday life. The Polish language still bore the marks of the Romantic era, which left it somewhat ethereal and ill adapted to the reality of the twentieth century. French influence can be detected in a colony of Polish poets and painters who lived in Paris during the years 1908–1912, but only a new generation of poets, making their debut after the war, would be ready to translate and absorb the influence of poets like Rimbaud.

In French poetry a reaction against the "purity" advocated by Mallarmé came around 1913, not without some borrowing from Walt Whitman and his French translator, Valery Larbaud (1881–1957), who in his *Barnabooth* introduced a poetry of avid absorption of the world, cosmopolitan in its subject matter and descriptive. Travel also informed the poetry of Blaise Cendrars (1887–1961), who tried to describe landscapes with photographic exactness. Cendrars's "Easter in New York" appeared in 1913, the same year as "Zone," the poem of Paris by his friend Guillaume Apollinaire (1880–1918). Who influenced whom in these works remains an open question. These two poets represent a high point in modern French poetry, which has, however, chosen the Mallarméan path of condensing, distilling, and refining the language in search of a "pure lyricism."

7   *A stand-in / For religion, and such it will remain*: This art for art's sake was created by writers who were for the most part agnostics or atheists and replaced religion with an art that built its own "supreme fictions," to use the expression of Wallace Stevens, an American poet in the Mallarméan line.

8   *Kasprowicz roared, tore at the silken tethers*: Jan Kasprowicz (1860–1926), acclaimed as the leading poet of Young Poland (there was at this time also a Young Germany, a Young Scandinavia, etc.), struggled in vain with the prevailing style of Polish poetry, which resembled, in some respects, the English of Swinburne. A peasant by origin, self-taught, a voracious reader, he learned foreign languages and translated from them, not very successfully. In his own poetry the daring idea of transposing the Catholic hymns sung in Polish country churches falls short of expectations. The poems are verbose. Nor does his *Book of the Poor,* a collection of religious poems written in simple "homely" quatrains, seem of lasting value. He remains as an example of an honorably lost battle with an inherited style. To his credit I should add that he did not strive for purity; he wanted to put his verse in the service of his own peasant religious sensitivity.

8   *Leopold Staff was the color of honey*: This was a time of a desperate revision of traditional religious values, and of the

spell of Friedrich Nietzsche's writings, which were appearing in Polish translation. Another name pronounced with reverence in those days was that of the pessimistic philosopher Arthur Schopenhauer. No wonder that Polish modernist poetry was gloomy in tone. Leopold Staff (1878–1957), on the contrary, conquered his readers by his praise of life, of the sun, of human will. His work, read in chronological order, illustrates several decades of changes in the language and in literary technique. Though he used metrical form and rhyme for most of his life (even after 1918, when most Polish poets had begun to abandon them), in his old age, after the Second World War, under the influence of younger poets, he completely liberated his verse from traditional forms. His few, brief, concise poems of that period are his masterpieces.

Versification, as is well known, depends upon the nature of a given language. Polish has a stable accent which falls on the penultimate syllable of every word (as in Italian). Its syllabic verse is modeled on the medieval Latin of the Church and tends to generate a line of two groups of syllables, separated by a medial caesura: either five syllables plus seven syllables, or six syllables followed by six. The present "treatise" makes use of five plus six, but without rhyme. Most Polish poets have, without regret, bid farewell to the corset of regular patterns. Their Russian colleagues, however, are still bound by the clearly audible beat in their language, which has a movable accent.

Leopold Staff's vocation seemed to be as a transitional poet. The mannerisms of his diction, typical of Young

Poland, gradually disappeared, though he achieved this simplicity only late in life.

8   *As to Leśmian, he drew his own conclusions*: The style and diction of the Young Poland poets damaged their reputations. This explains the strange case of Bolesław Leśmian (1878–1937). He quite consciously used the mannerisms of his time for his own purposes, writing his fairy tales in verse in a folkish idiom. Behind this facade was hidden the skeptical philosophy of a man well-read in anthropology and the history of religion, especially the religions of India. The action of his poems takes place on earth and in heaven; the poems abound in shapes and colors, but they are "irreal." His style spoke for classifying him as a relic of Young Poland, and by the interwar years when the style of Young Poland belonged to the past, he was thought of as a good but minor poet. Fortunately for him, he died in 1937, for he was a Jew and would otherwise have perished at the hands of the Nazis. By the 1960s and 1970s, he was rediscovered as a major poet of the Polish language.

8   *Two boys lived not far from one another*: These two boys who lived on the same street were Józef Konrad Korzeniowski (1857–1924), known to the world as Joseph Conrad, and Stanisław Wyspiański, the reformer of the Polish theater, already mentioned in my commentary.

Conrad attended St. Ann's High School, by reputation one of the best in the city. A nonchalant and unruly youth, he spent much of his time reading. Polish Romantic literature was a mainstay of the curriculum and Polish readers are able to detect traces of its impact in his plots and characters. Wyspiański was the son of a sculptor, who had his workshop in that street. The son studied painting at the Kraków Academy of Fine Arts, then for a while in Paris. He repaid his native city with the magnificent stained glass panels in St. Francis's Church. But his main preoccupations were theater and poetry. His plays in verse, especially *The Wedding, Liberation, Acropolis,* and *November Night,* belong to the permanent repertory of Polish theater. Practically incomprehensible to a foreigner, they are webs of allusions to the history of the country and in this they can be compared to some plays of the Irish playwrights.

8   *He walked slowly up the marble stairs*: The scene is based on Conrad's letters. It is the momentous occasion on which he received an assignment as the captain of a steamboat in the Congo. His story "Heart of Darkness" (1902), written out of that experience, has been called (by Thomas Mann) the work that opens the twentieth century.

9   *also a puppet theater,/The same for centuries*: The Christmas puppet show gave Wyspiański a model for the structure of his *Wedding.*

9   *Dreamed of a national theater, as in Greece*: Wyspiański did not rely only on his intuitions. He turned to the ancient Greek tragedies as an example of the deep bond that existed between the actions on a stage and the life of a community.

(High schools at that time taught a good deal of Latin and Greek.) He strove to create a monumental theater in which the problems of the nation could be discussed through symbolic transpositions.

9 *He couldn't overcome the contradiction*: How to assess Wyspiański fairly? In his short life, filled with feverish artistic activity, he accomplished much, as a painter, a set designer, and a playwright. His plays, addressed to the intelligentsia, called for breaking the magic circle of political apathy—that dance of phantoms to the tune played by the straw man in *The Wedding*. And soon enough, in the wake of the outbreak of war, his appeal was heard. He revolutionized the Polish stage and created "the art of theater," featuring the director of the spectacle as the central figure. And yet he paid a price for being born in a time that was not, because of the literary style of Young Poland, especially propitious for poets. His visions and his linguistic means were in contradiction; his language was somewhat stilted and the problems of the intelligentsia of his time have receded into the past. Polish poets have not recognized him as their master or ancestor.

10 *As heritage we received another monument*: For sheer pleasure Krakóvian poets and painters organized a cabaret, the "Green Balloon," for which the poets wrote comic song lyrics while the painters adorned the walls with caricatures of popular personalities in the city. Especially funny were the verses of Tadeusz Żeleński (1874–1941), who used the

pseudonym "Boy." Published as *Słówka* (*Little Words*), his songs, irreverent, slightly obscene, spiced with vulgarisms from the street, were a turning point in the battle against the lofty language of Young Poland. Żeleński, a medical student, later a physician, became an important personality in Polish letters. Well educated, perfectly acquainted with French literature, he started to translate it, having found in Rabelais an earthiness and a dose of sex that served as a useful antidote to Polish writers' melancholic ruminations on the soul. Gradually he developed a plan to translate the canonical works of French literature and proved to be a brilliant and inventive re-creator, rather than translator, of those works. He accomplished a monumental oeuvre by this labor of love and talent. He also became known as a literary critic and scholar. Together with other Polish intellectuals, he was executed by the Nazis in 1941.

10   *On Oleandry field the locks of the carbines*: Some young men in Kraków were engaged in private military training. They came mostly from the intelligentsia and included poets and painters. They looked for an opportunity to act and found an organizer and commander in the person of Józef Piłsudski (1867–1935). Born in Lithuania—at that time part of the tsarist Empire—the son of a Polish-speaking, landowning family, he became a socialist and a professional revolutionary. Considered particularly dangerous by the tsarist authorities, he was arrested and served a term of exile in Siberia. The goal of his revolutionary activities was the liberation of Poland. Analyzing the international politi-

cal scene, he came to the conclusion that war was inevitable and that it was necessary to raise a military force to fight on the side of Austria against the Russians. He trained his followers on fields outside the city. As he foresaw, the war broke out, and in August 1914, at the head of his small legion, he marched to the front from Oleandry field in Kraków. Later, grown in number and seasoned in battle, his legion became the nucleus of the Polish Army. In 1918, with the end of the war, Piłsudski achieved his goal, an independent Poland.

10 *And she, she wears a lilac-colored veil*: The color lilac was fashionable, as was a small veil covering the upper part of the face. It was attached to a hat. The song she sings is authentic and not unrelated to the fates of those young frequenters of cafés who were changed into soldiers.

2. THE CAPITAL

13 *You, alien city on a dusty plain, / Under the cupola of the Orthodox cathedral*: The action of the poem moves to Warsaw. That city by the Vistula River is situated on a vast plain of mostly sandy soil that runs from the Carpathian Mountains to the Baltic Sea. It led for centuries the rather undistinguished life of a half-rural settlement. Fields near the city began to be used, however, as the location for massive gatherings of the gentry on the occasion of the election of the king (an institution peculiar to Poland). In 1596 the capital of Poland was moved there from Kraków, and since that mo-

ment the history of the city has mirrored the troubles of the country. Taken by the Swedes in 1656 and retaken by the Poles. Besieged by the Russians in 1794 and surrendering only after Suvorov's troops massacred ten thousand civilians from the suburb of Praga. Napoléon entered the city in 1806 and made it capital of the Duchy of Warsaw, which was to provide him with soldiers in his war against Russia. After his defeat, the city served as the capital of a truncated Kingdom of Poland under the sovereignty of Russia, whose autocratic ruler was at the same time the constitutional king of Poland, an awkward arrangement which led to the uprising of 1830, dethronement of the tsar-king, and war with Russia. That was, for a long time, the end of Polish statehood, and Warsaw was reduced to the status of the center of a province called By-Vistula. After a hopeless uprising in 1863, the very name of Poland could not be spoken, schools were Russified, students forbidden to speak their native language. Warsaw became a garrison town. To leave a permanent monument to its dominance, Russia built in the central square of the city an enormous Orthodox cathedral, which served only its own troops: the population was predominantly Roman Catholic.

Debased, humiliated, and Russified, the city became "alien" to many Poles. The old Polish-Lithuanian Commonwealth was multilingual, and the spread of the Polish language eastward had resulted in large Polish-speaking communities with capitals of their own, Wilno (today Vilnius) in Lithuania and Lwow (Lviv) in the Ukraine. These cities hardly looked toward Warsaw; they were oriented to Kraków, where under Austrian rule Polish schools and universities functioned, and books and newspapers were published under relatively mild censorship.

13 *The Cavalry Guard was your soldier of soldiers*: This passage of the poem uses Russian expressions difficult to translate. "Allaverdy" was a bawdy song that had originated in the Caucasus and was sung by drunken Russian officers. The Cavalry Guards were elite troops of the tsar's empire.

13 *To your grief and debauchery and misery*: The poverty of the population and the large number of soldiers garrisoned in the city led inevitably to widespread prostitution. Officers billeted there enjoyed a "merry Warsaw," of ill fame, though the more refined among them also sensed the hatred in the air.

13 *An ensign elopes with a railwayman's daughter*: The reference is to an actual event. A girl of rare beauty, the daughter of a Polish railwayman, eloped with a young Russian ensign, who took her to Russia. Subsequently she married an American multimillionaire who bought her Le Théâtre des Champs-Elysées in Paris.

13 *At Czerniakowski Street, at Górna and Wola*: Fragments from two Warsaw street songs popular around the time of the First World War are telescoped here into three lines of

verse—which creates an insuperable obstacle to translation. I must add that Polish readers do not know the songs either. The streets named were in working-class neighborhoods full of cheap taverns. The "Black Mary" of the song was obviously liked for her carefree carousing.

13 *And you are ruled, City, from a citadel*: The tsarist authorities considered Warsaw a dangerous city, full of clandestine activities and uprisings. They built the citadel to control it.

13 *Cossack horses prick their ears*: The Cossacks were used against political demonstrations. The lyric comes from a socialist song.

13 *How could you become the capital of a state*: At the beginning of World War I German troops advanced east very rapidly. The front line passed through Byelorussia and the Ukraine. Warsaw remained in German hands until November 1918, when the Germans, defeated by the Allies in the west, departed. Independent Poland, with Warsaw as its capital, was proclaimed on November 11, 1918.

13 *Crowded with refugees from the Ukraine*: There was a large Polish-speaking population in the Ukraine, many of whom fled to Warsaw to escape civil war and revolution.

14 *A saber, rifles from French army surplus*: The war between Poland and the Soviet army was very unpopular in the capi-

tals of Europe. As a result, the Polish army had difficulty acquiring arms and was poorly equipped. Because the Russian Revolution was considered socialist and progressive, strikes were organized in many cities to stop the flow of supplies to Poland. The battle of 1920, fought at the gates of Warsaw, won by Poland, barred the Soviet way to Germany and probably prevented the creation of a Communist state there.

14 *They don't know that, one day, harsh brasses will play/The "Internationale" above their graves*: Soviet troops entered Warsaw twenty-five years later, in January 1945, and established a Communist government. Many former anti-Soviet militants were destined to serve the new rulers.

14 *Yet you exist. With your blackened ghetto*: At the center of Warsaw was a neighborhood inhabited by Jews who dressed in black and were mostly very poor.

14 *He could never believe in permanence*: The creator of independent Poland and chief of the newly restored state was Józef Piłsudski. He tried and failed to create an independent Ukraine to protect Poland from the east, but he won the Battle of Warsaw. He was obsessed with the possibility of attack, both from the east and the west. His fears materialized after his death in 1935 in the form of the 1939 pact between Stalin and Hitler, which partitioned the country between the two powers.

14 *Till not one stone, O city, remains/Upon a stone*: Warsaw was to-
tally destroyed in 1944. At the end of World War II no
other European city presented a view of such total ruin.
Some streets were bombed during the siege of Warsaw in
1939, others in the German action against the ghetto upris-
ing of 1943, and whole neighborhoods were burned to the
ground in the uprising of the Home Army in 1944. Total
devastation was inflicted when Hitler, after the battles in
the city had died out, ordered that Warsaw be "razed with-
out a trace"—by dynamiting the houses street by street.

15 *Your ramparts will be built by poets*: In a country whose history
is rich in tragedy—assaults by powerful neighbors, foreign
occupation, uprisings against occupations—poetry fulfilled
the special function of an invisible government and was
honored as such.

15 *A poet needs, first, to issue from good stock*: I speak here of a
group of poets called "Skamander" after a magazine they
started after World War I. They came from the intelligentsia
and were the first generation of poets of urban origin in a
basically rural country. Their origins reflected the ethnic
mix of Poland. Julian Tuwim (1894–1953) descended from
progressive Jewish intellectuals of the city of Łódź. Jan
Lechoń (1899–1956), family name Leszek Serafinowicz,
came from burghers of Armenian origin. Antoni Słonim-
ski (1895–1976) counted among his ancestors a Jewish sci-
entist and Jewish inventors, as well as medical doctors.
Jarosław Iwaszkiewicz (1894–1980) came from the Polish

intelligentsia in the Ukraine. Kazimierz Wierzyński (1894–1969) was of German ancestry. United by friendship and mutual appreciation, they conquered the public and became the most highly regarded poets of the years between the wars.

15 *Noisy at the Picadore*: The Second World War and the ensuing political events were to separate friends. Tuwim succeeded in leaving Poland at the beginning of the war and heard from New York the news of his mother's death at the hands of the Nazis and of the mass murders that amounted to the end of Polish Jewry. He had always been a romantic revolutionary, and before the war at his poetry readings in small, predominantly Jewish towns he used to recite poems of the French Revolution ("*Ça ira*"). This is what is meant by "a sound belated by a hundred years." Most of his audiences perished in the Shoah. Those who survived left for Israel or Western countries. Some of those who remained threw in their lot with the Communist state.

15 *The ball at the Senator goes on and on*: This is an allusion to a ball famous in Polish literature. In *Forefathers' Eve*, by Adam Mickiewicz (1798–1855), Poland's national poet, a high Russian official in an occupied Polish city gives a ball which the reluctant Polish elite is expected to attend. Tuwim returned to Poland in 1946, convinced that only the spread of Communism could build a rampart against Fascism, which had found its perfect incarnation in the Nazi movement. Basically, however, Tuwim felt horror when he meditated

on any human society. Anarchism lay in the deepest layers of his creative work.

15 *Lechoń-Herostrates trampled on the past*: In his youth, in 1918, Lechoń wrote a poem titled "Herostrates," in which he identified with a Greek from Ephesus who set fire to the temple of Diana there in 350 B.C. The poem was an outburst of joy at a new era. The long foreign occupation of Poland was over at last and with it the duties of the poet as a fighter for freedom. Now he was free to write on subjects dear to poets at all times. "In the spring," he wrote, "let me see spring, not Poland." By an irony of fate, Lechoń's destiny was to idealize Old Poland and to appoint himself the guardian of "true Polishness" and of the traditional attachment to "God and Country." He was in Paris at the outbreak of the Second World War, became a political émigré in New York, and committed suicide there in 1956 by jumping from a skyscraper.

16 *Or on religion, Polish, not Catholic*: For Lechoń, Roman Catholicism was primarily a national religion. His poems of piety do not probe very deeply the meaning of Christianity. Or-Ot was the pseudonym of Artur Oppman (1869–1931), a poet whose traditional rhymed syllabic verse was extolled by Lechoń.

16 *What of Słonimski, sad and noble-minded?*: Antoni Słonimski was, basically, a rationalist and a partisan of the scientific

world view. His belief in a happy human future based on the progress of rationality was ill adapted to his times. Yet he was brave. In his "Weekly Chronicle" in the weekly *Literary News,* he castigated absurd political ideas, reactionary slogans, and anti-Semitism. He was an admirer of H. G. Wells and, largely for that reason, an anglophile. His satirical writings are more admired than his poetry, which is didactic. Słonimski spent the war in London, but returned to Warsaw in 1950, only to join within a few years the liberal opposition against censorship and the violation of human rights.

16   *Iwaszkiewicz built his house of brilliant stones*: His biography is marked by the sudden turns history imposed on his generation. In his youth, the least appreciated of the Skamander poets because of his aestheticism, there were few admirers (I was one of them) for his musical verse, which was sensuous and rich in color. His translations of Rimbaud were a radical departure from earlier translations of that poet. The colors, shapes, and sounds in his writing show the impact on him of the Ukrainian landscapes among which he grew up. During the war Iwaszkiewicz stayed in Poland. His house near Warsaw was the center of underground cultural life and, occasionally, a refuge for people endangered by the Nazis, including many Jews. After Poland was "liberated" by the Soviet army and a government of Polish Communists installed, Iwaszkiewicz, though he had no illusions as to the character of the new regime, consciously chose the role of collaborator and allowed himself to be

used as a figurehead by the government's propaganda machine. However, he remained largely independent in his writings and in his work as an editor. He was, in a way, a sentimental patriot and would occasionally slip into populism.

16   *Not morally superior, just more proud*: This passage refers to Kazimierz Wierzyński who, during the Second World War and afterward, lived as a political émigré on the East Coast of America. Uncompromising, he never returned to Poland. His youthful poems are exuberant, in contrast to his later work.

17   *There had never been such a Pléiade!*: The younger generation recognized the exceptional gifts of the Skamander poets, who did in some ways resemble "La Pléiade," the famous coterie of the French Renaissance, but they also rebelled against the "flaw of harmony" in their poems.

17   *Tuwim lived in awe, twisted his fingers*: Julian Tuwim was, in fact, torn between his left leanings and metaphysical horror. His last words, scribbled on a napkin, were "For the sake of economy, extinguish the light eternal which was supposed to shine on me." This paraphrases a prayer for the dead in the Latin Mass: "And may the perpetual Light shine upon them."

18   *Nor did Broniewski win their admiration*: Władysław Broniewski (1897–1962) was a Communist poet whose verse

resembled, strangely enough, revolutionary songs of the nineteenth century.

19 *In the swarm of the Kraków avant-garde*: The Constructivist avant-garde had their home in Kraków where they published the magazine *Zwrotnica* ("The Switch") in the 1920s. They regarded metaphor as the basic building material of the poem. At the same time, they moved away from the poetry of personal feeling and strove for a kind of objectivity, rejected the metrical poetry of Skamander and searched for new rhythms. The most important among them, Julian Przyboś (1901–1970), was a rationalist, faithful to the worldview of modern science.

20 *Would spit when a crowd of screaming youths*: The universities were hotbeds of anti-Semitic activity. Their aggression was directed primarily against college students, but it would occasionally spill into the streets, and then Jewish merchants were attacked.

20 *The end was prepared in advance*: An Hegelian (or Marxist) proposition, in my opinion, of limited philosophical value. Should we assume that societies, if they are retrograde, are doomed by a mysterious Spirit of History. Poland was retrograde. It succumbed to the united forces of two military powers, Nazi Germany and the Soviet Union.

20 *Those who saw took refuge in irony*: Poland was ruled by a junta of colonels who fanned chauvinism and the martial spirit

to mask the public fear of an inevitably approaching war. Those who could see through the facade responded ironically. Or, rather, I, a commentator, should speak here in my own name, without recourse to generalization.

20 *One of those who understood pretended*: Can a poet remain detached while all around him people are animated by the same powerful nationalistic passion? Konstanty Ildefons Gałczyński (1905–1953) answered that question in the negative. As the extreme right dominated public opinion, he offered to it his considerable literary gifts and became its bard. He threatened liberals and radicals with "a night of long knives." After the war, which he survived in a POW camp, he became, however, the bard of Communist Poland. His instinct, or need, was to be where the masses were.

20– *Let it be stated here clearly: the Party/Descends directly from the*
21 *fascist Right*: Obóz Narodowo-Radkalny (O.N.R.) was the extreme rightist party. The Communist Party became its successor when it made its appeal to Polish nationalism.

21 *Gałczyński tied these elements together*: As in neighboring Nazi Germany, the Polish rightists were anti-philistine, populist, and racist. Horst Wessel was the author of the Nazi hymn. One may well ask how, in Poland, directly endangered by Germany, such an imitative movement was possible. Were these people blind? They were.

21 *Czechowicz, the bucolic, was quite different*: The leading poet of the new generation, Józef Czechowicz (1903–1939), was a friend of mine, and I try to describe his poetry, which is untranslatable, for it makes use of sonorities proper to one language only. He rejected regular meter and punctuation and followed his ear, which was sensitive to folk songs and Christmas carols, as well as to Polish bourgeois lyrics and dances of the seventeenth century. His poetry is undulant, subdued, close to dream. He was killed by a German bomb in September 1939 in his native city of Lublin, where he is buried.

21 *Not one nation but a hundred nations*: Lucjan Szenwald (1909–1944) became a Communist is his early youth. He was self-taught, but erudite, and translated poetry from English and ancient Greek. After the partition of Poland, he moved to the Soviet zone, underwent military training in Siberia, and became a political officer in the Red Army. He is the author of an ode to Mother Siberia. In 1944, when his unit was fighting in Poland, he was killed in an automobile accident.

22 *The book has a title: Afloat in the Forest*: The full title of that book for young people is *Afloat in the Forest, or a Voyage among the Treetops by Captain Mayne-Reid*. The first edition was published in 1889. Thomas Mayne-Reid (b. 1818) is an author not known today to American readers, but his books for young readers about a romanticized America were once

(together with those of the German writer Karl May) staple readings in many European countries, including Poland and Russia. Mayne-Reid led an adventurous life. Originally from northern Ireland, he migrated to America, where he worked as a teacher, a trapper, and a journalist. He distinguished himself in the war against Mexico. In the 1860s in New York he edited a magazine of adventure for young people called *Onward!* Later he moved to London and his books enjoyed great success. The book referred to here deals with adventures on the Amazon River.

22– *And, if he survives destruction, it is he/Who will preserve with ten-*
23 *derness his guides*: The author expresses in these lines his gratitude to his predecessors, poets whom he read in adolescence, including some less well-known names: Józef Wittlin (1896–1976), in his youth the author of expressionist verses on hunger; Stanisław Baliński (1899–1984), who published a slim volume of verse on Persia; Adam Ważyk (1905–1982), translator of Guillaume Apollinaire; as well as Maria Pawlikowska-Jasnorzewska (1893–1945), perhaps a Polish Sappho. "Ursula" was the daughter of a major Polish poet, Jan Kochanowski. Her untimely death is the subject of his best-known poem, "Laments." In one of Pawlikowska's poems, the recorded voice of Caruso complains, asking "*Perquè?*"

23 *Perhaps it was not for nothing, the soldier's blood*: Independent Poland of the years 1918–1939 owed its existence to the

sacrifice of life by many young men who served under Piłsudski and won the Battle of Warsaw in 1920.

23 *Piłsudski should not shoulder all the blame*—: He was often criticized for his capriciousness and his lack of interest in the internal affairs of the state. Irritated by the squabbling of the political parties in the Diet, which led to frequent changes of government, he made a putsch in 1926, and took for himself the part of "lord protector." His one interest was, in fact, protecting Poland's borders. His plan to protect them from the east by creating a federation with Lithuania and Byelorussia failed, as his attempt to capture Kiev and call into being an independent Ukraine failed. He was obsessed by the idea of an attack on Poland by its eastern and western neighbors, and his fears were not without foundation, as the 1939 pact between Hitler and Stalin demonstrated.

24 *It's we who create it every day anew*: We sustain the existence of the realm of poetry only through daily effort. It is wrested from the world not by negating the things of the world, but by respecting them more than we respect aesthetic values. That is the condition for creating valid beauty. If it is obtained too easily, it evaporates. This passage presents the principle of realistic poetics applied by the author in *A Treatise on Poetry*.

24 *The last poem of the epoch went to print*: Its author, Władysław Sebyła (1902–1940), belonged to a group around the maga-

zine *Kwadryga*. He rejected the poetics of Skamander, searching instead for a technique capable of expressing philosophic meanings. He was influenced by the patron saint of modern intellectual poetry, Cyprian Kamil Norwid (1821–1883), who, having been rejected by his contemporaries, was rediscovered, nearly two decades after his death in Paris in a hospice for the destitute. Sebyła was drafted at the beginning of the war and served as a non-commissioned officer. Taken prisoner by the Soviet army and interned in a POW camp, he was executed in the famous massacre of Polish officers in Katyn Woods near Smolensk in April 1940. The Polish prisoners executed that spring under Stalin's orders numbered 23,653.

The poem of Sebyła to which the line refers presents Poland as a rural country, defenseless and attached to its myth of origin under the rule of a peasant-king. Swiatowid, one of its pagan gods, had two faces, looking in opposite directions.

25 *Barrage balloons hang like ripened fruit*: This is a faithful description of the night preceding the outbreak of war, which started on September 1, 1939, with Hitler's dawn attack on Poland. In the original text, the "watchman on duty" is anonymous, but it is easy to guess that I speak of myself. In this translation, I changed "he" to "I."

This chapter deals with life under the Nazi occupation in Poland from 1939 to 1945. The onslaught of the German army was met at the line of the Bug River, in fulfillment of the Hitler-Stalin pact, by the Soviet army, putting an end to the existence of inter-war Poland. Its eastern provinces became part of the Soviet Union, while a Nazi administration was established in the west—with peculiar new lines of division: districts bordering Germany were simply included in the Reich, while for the rest a new administrative unity was created, the General Government. It was not a satellite state, as in the case of Slovakia or Croatia, since no puppet governing body existed. The whole was ruled by the governor, Hans Frank, who took up residence in Kraków. He was sentenced to death at Nuremberg for the crime of geno-cide.

The administrative arrangements in Poland reflected Nazi racialist theory, according to which inferior races should not be allowed self-rule. The Polish intelligentsia was to be liquidated, while the less educated classes would be employed in physical labor. Terror applied to the three-million-strong Jewish popula-tion indicated from the beginning that the Germans had pre-pared a "Final Solution." The new borders, carving Poland into several carefully guarded pieces, seemed an irrational idea, but they served to hamper the movements of population and cut off routes of escape.

The sudden defeat in September 1939 was a shock to the in-telligentsia. Of course, had Poland been ten times better armed, it could not have resisted two enemies at once. The fall of France a year later proved that even industrialized countries were unable to resist the German military machine. The defeat brought to the surface the obsolete character of Poland's social structure: it was a country of villages, with relatively few cities and manufacturing centers, unified by the people's nationalism and their ardent and ritualistic Roman Catholicism. Now, when all state institutions crumbled, was a time of particular nakedness and pitiless assessment. It amounted for many to a meeting with the twentieth century in its harshest form.

In the fall of 1940 the concentration camp of Oświęcim (Auschwitz) was created. It was not originally intended for Jews. Its first inmates were Poles, plucked at random from the streets as a measure of terror. That same autumn ghettoes for the Jews were designed and the Jewish population ordered to move there. Some neighborhoods were declared "for Germans only," and were thus forbidden to Poles. All this occurred in Europe, but a Europe overrun by an empire which was to last, according to Hitler, a thousand years. A poet, in whatever conquered country he lived, but especially in Poland, assigned himself two major tasks: first, not to succumb to despair; second, to try to grasp the causes of the total triumph of evil. *A Treatise on Poetry* describes scenes of everyday life during the occupation, which differed radically from that in most western European countries. At the same time it attempts to describe a mind in search of meaning.

29   *In Masovian forest, on needle-covered paths*: The Nazi administration introduced food rationing in the cities, but the rations allotted were not sufficient for survival. This led to high

prices and smuggling. Often peasant smugglers had to cross borders illegally between the new administrative regions, such as this border between territories incorporated into the Reich and those incorporated in the General Government. Shouting, occasionally shooting, the German police chased off hordes of smugglers, but their efforts to enforce the regulations were halfhearted, because if they had succeeded in interdicting the supply of food from the countryside, it would have reduced their own access to the black market.

29 *In the town, a bullet is carving a dry trace/In the sidewalk near bags of homegrown tobacco*: Black market goods, including tobacco, were usually displayed on the sidewalks and suddenly disappeared at the approach of a police patrol. The poem draws on scenes observed by the author. The death agony of an old man, Jewish, attracted no attention: that was part of the general callousness and indifference.

30 *Stanisław, or Henryk, sounds the bottom with a pole*: In summer the Vistula is shallow. Old-fashioned steamboats with paddle wheels had to move slowly, probing the bottom. "One meter" indicates the water level.

30 *The Spirit of History is out walking*: Is history just a mass of facts, without traceable logic or direction? Or is it submitted to hidden laws? That question had preoccupied thinkers since the early nineteenth century and was somehow connected to a belief in human progress. Georg Wil-

helm Friedrich Hegel's philosophy gave the idea of progress its trait of inevitability. According to Hegel, mankind, throughout its life in time, that is, in history, is pushed forward by the internal necessity of the human mind. History therefore is not chaos, and at every moment we may discern the actions of a Zeitgeist, a Spirit which pushes man to a higher stage of development. Hegel's conviction was inherited, of course, by Karl Marx, who assigned a decisive role to economics. In conquering Europe, did Hitler have the Spirit of History on his side? After a relatively short period of democracy, was totalitarianism the next inevitable phase of human development? In Poland the temptation to succumb to Nazi ideology was nil, since the Poles knew that, after the Jews, Hitler targeted them as among the historical refuse to be swept aside. The attraction of Communism, of the philosophical Hegelian-Marxist variety, was another matter. Given the destruction of institutions, mores, and values in Nazi Europe, a return to the capitalist system and political democracy characteristic of the prewar years seemed totally improbable.

30   *He whistles, he likes these countries washed/By a deluge, deprived of shape and now ready*: Underground literary circles were inclined to socialism, but not certain that the Spirit of History favored Communism in its Soviet form. Belief in progress excluded the possibility of the Nazis' ultimate victory; it was contrary to several centuries of European values. But if National Socialism razed the fields, what did History intend for them?

30 *Under his palm, a rider on a bicycle*: This passage attempts to capture, in a sarcastic shortcut, the political panorama. Beneath the surface of the occupation, Polish institutions were reconstructed and amounted to an underground state. At the head stood the council of political parties and a delegate to the Polish government in exile in London. The prewar army became the clandestine Home Army. All this testified to a Polish gift for improvisation and confirmed the German opinion that the Polish intelligentsia were implacable enemies. Attempts on the lives of German officials had earned Poland a reputation as a dangerous place. The poet, however, stresses the durability of prewar class divisions—the manor, the boys in officers' boots, the journeymen.

This poem takes as its subject poetry, not politics. Part three tries to answer the question of how to save poetry, save its very existence. After the war, the German philosopher Theodor Adorno asked if poetry was possible after Auschwitz. Here a similar concern is visible. *A Treatise on Poetry* asks the same question, not in the abstract, but in relation to the past of Polish poetry: whether its future, if it had one, needed to be thought of in terms of continuity or rebellion. And since that poetry had always been marked by the history of the country, options in poetics could not be separated from political options.

In the whole debate about the Spirit of History, it would seem that the following premise is detectable. Human societies live enveloped in myths and legends. Sometimes these myths and legends serve as a positive function, but they become harmful when they obscure reality. History, its Spirit, does not favor those who refuse to examine reality in its nakedness. An example of a society entangled in delusion was Nazi Germany. Observation of German behavior in Poland led inevitably to the conclusion that the Nazis were doomed to defeat, precisely because their inhuman racial doctrine and its cruelties were perpetrated against their own interests.

The narrator assumes that there is a certain level of awareness of reality below which no real poetry can be accomplished. A poet should not be the prisoner of national myths. A Nazi poet (they existed) was a contradiction in terms. But what about a patriotic Polish poet in a country fighting for its survival? The government in exile in London and its underground state meant a continuation of prewar Poland, both its mentality and its poetry. A break with that poetry, a new beginning, amounted to distancing oneself from the rhetoric of the underground state. A new poetry, intellectual and ironic, might be able to cope with atrocity and the sense of absurdity. So this chapter describes a breakthrough in Polish poetry which can be dated roughly to 1943. After the end of hostilities, that new poetry would play its own game, distancing itself from the language of the new rulers, that is, the Communists.

The mysterious link between poetry and politics is complex, difficult to analyze, yet its existence was understood by many twentieth-century poets who had analogous experiences in their own countries during these years of war and revolution. It meant that a mental act, securing a grasp on reality, preceded the poetic act, if the poem, however noble its intention, was not to be mere words.

31   *Who does not acknowledge him begins to mumble*: If we assume that the Spirit of History dooms all those who cling to the past at any price (an unproved proposition), the poet who aligns himself with the forces of reaction will "mumble." In practice, refusing this option meant an unwillingness to write the sort of patriotic poetry that appeared in innumerable underground publications. The London émigré government, and most Poles, believed, against all evidence, that Poland would be liberated by the Western Allies. The alliance between Russia and the West was ambiguous: but in the end it meant paying Russia for the defeat of Germany with half of Europe and contributing to the rise of a Communist empire. Was this a trick of the Spirit of History? Had not Marx proclaimed that the end of capitalism was inevitable? Was not this the moment when his prophecy began to be fulfilled? Yet the poet, if he recognized the "historical necessity" of Communism, abdicated his role, which depended on not being seduced by any social or political system.

31   *Bright ladies, princes with consorts, where are you?*: A new era in the relation of the poet to society was approaching. Once, in the Middle Ages and the Renaissance, he could be rewarded for his art by flattering the aristocracy. Left to him-

self in a democracy, he did not fare very well. And now an omnipotent Communist state would need his "flesh and blood," his total commitment.

31 *Do we know you as the Spirit of the Earth*: In Goethe's *Faust* the Spirit of the Earth was Nature, which governed with the law of universal necessity. If the Spirit of History is just another name for the Earth Spirit, then the law of necessity, of strict determinism, applies to history as well. The poem thus enters into a realm of insoluble philosophical problems. In its treatment of our human species as part of nature, the impact of biological science on the mind of the narrator is apparent. In practice these questions change into another: should we think of historical cataclysms as we think of natural disasters? What then is a dignified human response to a political system that claims to be inevitable? Darwinism influenced both Nazism and Marxism. In the first, the survival of the fittest was interpreted racially; in the second, in terms of social classes.

32 *Clandestine bulletins in a green bag*: The underground press in occupied Poland was a phenomenon unique in Europe, both for its wide circulation and for the number of its printing shops. It reflected a large spectrum of political opinions, including those of the right and the extreme right. This did not happen in other countries where the extreme right collaborated with the Nazis. The press, with the exception of a few Communist leaflets, recognized the exiled government in London as the expression of Poland's

will to fight. The Communist network, identified in public opinion with Moscow, was weak.

32 *For punishment I took away their reason*: A reader of the clandestine press could not but remain skeptical about its truthfulness. Designed to boost morale and to keep the temperature of nationalism high, it hid unpleasant facts about Allied-Soviet cooperation, which would have undermined the belief that the Allies would ultimately liberate Poland. Fear of Moscow was great. To accept the idea that liberation might come from Russia was to despair.

32 *With what word to defend human happiness*—: A realistic assessment of the situation left no doubt about the preeminence of Communism in postwar Europe. A poet could not stop thinking about his poetics in terms of its usefulness in the encounter with Marxism.

33 *The poem of propaganda will not last*: The number of patriotic anti-Nazi poems was astronomical. Useful at a given moment, they served the purpose of inciting heroic resistance, but their artistic life was short.

33 *The twenty-year-old poets of Warsaw*: This was a generation of poets who were children when the war broke out. They grew up in conditions of terror and indigence, took courses at a clandestine university, started to write poems and copied them with primitive techniques. Their story is heroic, heartrending, and absurd. Their small review *Art*

and Nation voiced the ideology of Polish nationalism ("Imperial Poland"). Its editors perished one by one, in Auschwitz, in street executions, in combat. To their elder colleagues, including the narrator of this poem, it was obvious that their nationalist passion was the obverse of German nationalist passion and was tainted by the same folly. Their thinking, however, was a revival of Polish romanticism, with its messianic overtones which stressed the redeeming value of selflessly sacrificing one's life for one's country. They not only wrote and edited, they underwent military training and were convinced of their imminent deaths in combat.

And they were gifted. They present today's literary scholars with a puzzle. They perished; their verses and their deaths made them mythical figures, yet they built no bridge between the past and the future. Their sensibility testifies to the survival of an eerie Polish romanticism from the beginning of the nineteenth century, and in that way they mark a short-lived regression. In their forms they were not indebted to Skamander, though they practiced a mostly rhymed and metrical poetry. Their metaphors were influenced by the prewar avant-garde. But postwar Polish poetry did not follow in their footsteps. The difference in ideology was too radical.

34 *Copernicus: the statue of a German or a Pole?:* A statue of Nicolaus Copernicus, seated, a globe in his hand, stands in the center of Warsaw. It bears an inscription in Polish: "To

Copernicus—Compatriots." The Germans erased the inscription and replaced it with one in German. In fact, Copernicus lived at a time when the modern notion of nationality did not exist. He studied at the Jagiellonian University in Kraków, wrote in Latin, was a subject of the Polish king. What happened on May Day in 1943 can serve as an example of the absurdity inherent in nationalism outbidding nationalism. Three poets, from the group in question, decided to lay flowers in the national colors at the foot of the monument. It was a students' prank. An exchange of shots with the German police ensued and one of them, Wacław Bojarski, was mortally wounded.

35 *Trzebiński, the new Polish Nietzsche*: Andrzej Trzebiński (1922–1943) was brilliant, especially as an essayist. He belonged to the extreme right. Although the narrator of the poem pays him tribute, he strongly disliked his way of thinking. Trzebiński had no time to mature. Arrested by the Gestapo, he died in one of the numerous street executions. The victims, before being shot, had their mouths plastered shut.

35 *Baczyński's head fell against his rifle*: Krzysztof Kamil Baczyński (1921–1944) is today a well-known name in Poland. He did not belong to the *Art and Nation* group and, in fact, opposed them. In his short life he underwent an evolution from Marxism-Trotskyism to romantic-Messianic Christianity. Asthmatic, of frail health, he became a disci-

plined soldier of the Home Army by sheer effort of will. He was killed on a barricade during one of the first days of the Warsaw Uprising of 1944.

35 *Gajcy, Stroiński were raised to the sky*: Tadeusz Gajcy (1922–1944) is considered, together with Baczyński, the most gifted poet among his contemporaries. His potential, of course, was greater than his achievement. He died just as his talent came into its own. In the Warsaw Uprising, together with a friend, the poet Zdzisław Stroiński (1921–1944), he was in an action in a neighborhood which was the scene of particularly fierce battles. The street changed hands several times. The Germans dug a tunnel, mined the building the poet's unit was defending, and blew it up. "On the shield of an explosion": in ancient Greece the emblem of heroic death.

35 *Under a linden tree, as before, daylight*: The poem pauses to reflect for a moment on the poetry of older times, sustained by religious faith in a divine order. The linden tree calls to mind a poem written by Jan Kochanowski, who used to write under its shade when, after his travels through Italy and France, he settled on his country estate.

35 *Amid thunder, the golden house of* is/*Collapses*: The image of the world, as conceived by the Christian Middle Ages, was static. It was a world of eternal essences and their very being was the object of contemplation. The name of God, according to Thomas Aquínas, was equivalent to *esse*, to be-

ing itself. The disintegration of essences and the discovery of movement came gradually, culminating in the belief in universal evolution. For human societies, and also for art, the consequences of that change were enormous. One of them was that man started to look with nostalgia to a lost, golden house of being. The clash between the static and dynamic principles acquired for some Polish thinkers a political meaning. That was the view of the philosopher Józef Maria Hoene-Wroński (1778–1853), according to whom the struggle between the conservative force of *être* ("to be") and the revolutionary force of *devenir* ("to become") has been tearing Europe apart since the French Revolution.

36 *Now He, expected, for a long time awaited, / Raised up the smoke of a thousand censers*: The Warsaw Uprising began on August 1, 1944. No one, including its commanders, expected that the battles would last until October 2, 1944. It could be described as the clash of two principles, as understood by Hoene-Wroński. The Polish government in exile and its army represented the principle of *être*, namely, a return to prewar Poland. The Red Army was approaching the gates of the city. The Polish commanders hoped to take the city from the Germans before the Soviets arrived and greet the Russians as masters of their own home. Stalin, however, had different plans. He had created a puppet government of his own and he aimed to establish it in Warsaw. That summer the Soviet offensive stopped on the east bank of the Vistula, giving the Germans time to bring up reinforcements and retake Warsaw street by street from insurgents

desperately waiting for Soviet help. When they were defeated, the Soviet offensive resumed.

The Warsaw Uprising is considered the greatest tragedy in the history of Poland. It cost some 200,000 lives, military and civilian, and the complete destruction of the city. Columns of smoke, from bombs and heavy artillery, rose above the wreckage, hence "the smoke from a thousand censers." The tragedy had a demoralizing effect. It seemed to suggest that the reactionaries always made the wrong assessment and gave an inevitability to the Communist victory. In fact, the commanders of the resistance were trapped: if they had not acted, Stalin would have accused them of only feigned resistance to the Germans. The success was his, and the plan to rule Poland through his cadre of devoted Polish Communists was simplified by the destruction of the opposition.

36   —"*King of the centuries, ungraspable Movement*: This hymn is sung by those who opted for the power of *devenir*, universal movement, and against the power of *être*, being. They were now ready perhaps to enter the Communist party and become obedient servants of the Spirit of History.

37   *So they forswore. But every one of them*: Communist rule in Poland enforced the new order, but halfheartedly. The number of those who believed in historical necessity was limited. The worst years, the years of open terror, were 1949–1953. Poets were the first to profit from the liberalization after Stalin's death and the first to deviate from

Stalinist dogma. They had soon restored to poetry the right of detachment and dispassionate description.

37   *When they put a rope around my neck*: In speaking of the Shoah, stress is usually put on the destruction, not the life of the communities destroyed. Polish Jews had behind them a long and rich tradition of religious writing, art, architecture, and traditions of self-rule. In the interwar years their cultural life thrived. They created a network of schools with instruction in Yiddish and Hebrew and Polish, published a multitude of newspapers of various political orientations, created a Yiddish theater, formed sports clubs, built hospitals and orphanages. The majority spoke Yiddish, which contributed to a protracted debate about language in school. The Zionists pressed for Hebrew, assimilationists for Polish, socialists for preserving the Yiddish of the working classes. The Polish language was adopted by a considerable number and there were even Zionist Polish-language newspapers. It was also a time when the leading figures in Polish literature and theater and art were Jewish. Poland was, however, plagued by anti-Semitic movements of the extreme right. The first president of independent Poland, Gabriel Narutowicz, accused of having been elected by "the Jewish vote," was assassinated by a nationalist fanatic in 1922.

The Jewish community was strongly diversified. It had its wealthy at the very top and its masses living in dismal poverty. The Germans usually chose to locate the ghettoes in the poorest Jewish neighborhoods. In Poland the Shoah amounted to the extermination of a whole nation of Polish Jews. It was not one event among others. The shock left durable psychological and moral traces. The passage of time seems to change nothing in this respect. On the contrary, the Polish Jews are still vividly present in their absence.

37 *When they give me an injection of phenol*: Phenol is a chemical compound derived from benzene. It was used by the Nazis in the concentration camps to kill the weaker prisoners.

39 *Winter will end*: This small lyric is Jewish in origin; its author is anonymous. The author of this poem came across it in a short story by the Polish Jewish writer Artur Sandauer. Its ironic fatalism acquired new meaning because of succeeding events.

40 *Pickled cucumbers in a sweating jar*: The poem returns to the image of rural Poland, a great plain of villages and fields. Its main city, Warsaw, has been destroyed; the Jewish shtetls are nonexistent. It is as if it had returned to the conditions of a couple of centuries earlier, when there were the same cucumbers, the same hoes and baskets, and potatoes were dug by hand.

40 *Light Nanking silk our shoulders adorn*: In the narrator's memory fragments of old poems appear. In that devastated country he tries to recuperate the glorious moments of his culture. This quatrain comes from a poem by Adam

Mickiewicz written in 1818, "Winter in the City." Humorous, descriptive, it is written in the classical eighteenth-century style.

41   *Say what you desire/Tell us your hungers and your thirsts*: These lines are taken from Mickiewicz's verse drama *Forefathers' Eve*. They are pronounced by a shaman summoning the souls of the dead on All Souls' Day, a rite mixing Christian and pagan elements.

41   *No need for the bitterness of mustard seed*: To one of the souls, too happy in this life, the shaman announces, sententiously, that those who have not tasted the bitterness of earth will not taste the sweetness of Heaven.

41   *Poetry is well served by warm porcelains*: This line and the following six slightly rewrite lines taken from Mickiewicz's poetry. For a Polish reader, the playful use of these motifs is obvious. The "essences distilled from classical herbs" refers to the classical education which was assumed, among the Polish upper classes, to be the foundation of poetry: Latin, the Greek authors, and the Bible.

41   *What we do need are forests, clear waters*: If the first condition for practicing poetry was a classical education, the second was an appropriate geography. No important poets in Poland came from the monotonous plain in its center. Mickiewicz was a native of the much more picturesque Lithuania.

42   *As one scans the faces in a crowd of strangers*: A nostalgic avowal
     by the author who was, like his master Mickiewicz, born in
     Lithuania, and had never grown used to plains.

42   *Mickiewicz is too difficult for us*: Here the peasants speak. The
     heritage of the gentry and the Jews is alien to them.

42   *Ho la ho la*: The author does not go directly to the folklore,
     but makes use of Christmas carols arranged by the avant-
     garde poet Tytus Czyżewski (1883–1945) who drew from
     folk music in his poetry as composers like Béla Bartók and
     Karol Szymanowski did in their music. These fragments are
     taken from Czyżewski's "Pastorłki" ("Pastorals"), pub-
     lished in 1925. Christmas carols in Poland date mostly from
     the seventeenth century. They were strongly influenced by
     the baroque music of the Church. In his having recourse to
     them, one can guess the author's need, out of despair, to
     find some refuge in peasant culture. Unfortunately, the pas-
     torals are onomatopoeic and difficult to render in English.

44   *And why not a tinderbox with flint?*: Perhaps, in the midst of gen-
     eral devastation and a return to the primitive, a tinderbox
     would be more appropriate than matches. The narrator is tak-
     ing a rest from his agricultural occupation: digging potatoes.

4. NATURA

The narration moves from devastated wartime Poland to the
United States. This corresponds to the biography of the author,

who after the war served for several years as a member of the pro-Communist Polish Embassy in Washington, D.C. Whereas in the preceding chapter the narrator was confronted with historical events and political decisions, here he tries to forget for a moment Europe in the grip of its own demonic forces and to recover some equilibrium through looking at nature and its eternal rotation of seasons.

47 *Sunt mihi Dei Acherontis propitii!*: May the gods of Acheron favor me! The triple name of Jehovah be praised! Spirits of fire, of water, of earth, protect me!

Curiously enough, this magical incantation is taken from *Doctor Faustus* by Christopher Marlowe (1564–1593). Nature, however, does not respond, and no miraculous creature appears. Nature follows its own laws. Man, alien to Nature because of his mind, does not have at his disposal a magic spell.

48 The *Socrates of snails,* as he's been called,/*Musician of pears*: These epithets are borrowed from Wallace Stevens's "Comedian as the Letter C." Stevens stressed the ability of man to inhabit "supreme fictions" created by his mind.

48 *In sculptures and canvases our individuality/Manages to survive. In Nature it perishes*: Art is undoubtedly the manifestation of a human individual who puts his or her mark on an inimitable work. In Nature, on the contrary, it is the species, not the individual, that counts.

48   *Here there is sun. And whoever, as a child, / Believed*: It was my fancy as a child that grown-ups acted in the way that they did because they were unaware that the same actions had been performed in the same way by others before them. Does this apply also to lovemaking? Perhaps. Behind that childish notion was a belief in the power of human consciousness which should, theoretically, be able to change the order of things and move mountains. In other words, that child was ready to accept any miracle. Yet the repeatable pattern of things, as it turns out, is stronger than our desire for exception, and this is humiliating.

48   *Looks with wonder at the colors of the butterfly, / Inexpressible wonder, formless, hostile to art*: Colors and shapes in Nature are admirable, but they are basically alien to man and his art, which alone creates forms corresponding to his mind.

48   *To keep the oars from squeaking in their locks*: The author describes here a real event: how one evening on a lake in northern Pennsylvania he waited to see a beaver.

49   *It does not know time, hasn't heard of death*: An encounter with a beaver brings back a sense of the distance separating man from Nature. Consciousness, and therefore the awareness of belonging to a mortal species, builds a bar between man and other living beings. Yet precisely because of consciousness, power over other creatures is given to human beings.

49 *I remember everything. That wedding in Basel*: Memory enables man to connect to the past. Not just the memory of what happened to an individual, but the memory of the species. In other words, man possesses history and is able to embrace with his imagination events that occurred five hundred or five thousand years ago. The images in literature, painting, sculpture, film bring to life past epochs and millennia. This passage is like a description of a Renaissance painting and was possibly influenced by a painting.

50 *Perhaps this is only my own love speaking*: Identification with that bride from another epoch leads to personal reminiscence, to "the grit of subjectivity." The author is not fond of "confessional" poetry and only from time to time introduces events from his private life.

50 *Splash of a beaver in the American night*: Especially in his encounter with Nature, the author feels he is full of images from the pasts of various civilizations. History dwells in him, as do scenes and the names of bygone people, "Belinda of the big foot, Julia, Thaïs." This enumeration of women's names imitates François Villon's: "Where are the snows of yesteryear?"

51 *Peace to the princesses under the tamarisks*: An allusion to a French poem by Oscar Milosz, "Karmomama." It was inspired by a statuette of an Egyptian princess of that name in the Louvre, and is full of tenderness and pity.

51   *We are both the snake and the wheel*: We are live creatures like the snake and thus part of the kingdom of Nature. But we built the wheel that crushes the snake; we also belong to a different order, that of memory and consciousness.

51   *Time lifted above time by time*: This line refers to T. S. Eliot's "Burnt Norton" in *The Four Quartets*. Perhaps polemically, for the narrator seems not to aspire, as Eliot did, to arrival at an immobile point outside the passage of time. His intention is rather to humanize time.

51   *Before the butterfly and its color, he, numb,/Formless*: Man, as a part of Nature, is formless and unattainable to himself. He makes and grasps himself through myths and legends about himself, i.e., through an invisible plasma which he emanates and in which he envelops himself.

51   *For what is a butterfly without Julia and Thaïs?*: The world of Nature, palpable, accessible to our senses, provides us with material for thinking about human beings. Innumerable metaphors in love poems, for example, derive from plants, animals, birds, butterflies. Our kingdom and that of Nature are inseparable. And yet we simultaneously belong to it and do not.

51   *For how long will a nonsensical Poland*: These lines introduce a discussion of what the French language calls "*historicité*," the historical quality of phenomena. The English equivalent is "historicity." The notion became imperative in post-

war Poland, a country undergoing Marxist indoctrination. The narrator believes that Polish poetry should undergo a radical change as a precondition for meeting Marxist philosophy on its own ground. "A new diction" and "a new tenderness" are seen as the means of liberating man from fatalism and determinism, from the presumed law of historical necessity. The reasoning here is as follows: Marxism undermines all traditional values, including the idea of truth, by showing them to be historically contingent. All right, let us accept the challenge and plunge into historicity. Intense thinking about this prospect, however, leads in a different direction from the Marxist theses.

52 *Why cry out/That a sense of history destroys our substance*: A sense of history—an awareness that historicity is proper to all phenomena related to man—calls for a new skill in thinking about mankind. When we notice that the flow of time destroys our certainties by revealing their relative value, our first reaction is to retreat into the fortress of Being, to eternal and substantive ideas of the Good, the True, and the Beautiful, in order to protect ourselves from the corrosion of universal movement. In the third section of the poem the narrator spoke of the opposition between *être* and *devenir*. Here a similar opposition is discussed, and the conclusion is drawn that clinging to *être* (with political implications) is doomed to defeat sooner or later. The narrator's philosophical position is in some ways close to the pragmatism of Richard Rorty, though the poem was written long before Rorty's books appeared. The narrator is

convinced that his new, flexible way of thinking may serve to "rescue human beings" and to anticipate the future. "Keep, as in a seed, the unnamed future."

53   O City, O Society: The song (in rhymed quatrains) is addressed to society with its oppressive power over the individual. The city invoked is Paris. The author had lived there and would often take the suburban train from the station St.-Lazare. A girl in a window, seen from a passing train, unleashes in the narrator a desire to give human beings the freedom of which they are deprived, though they are not aware of it. The narrator here shows his colors as a socialist, though in his prophecy liberation would not be the result of a revolution on Marxist lines. He envisages victory as the moment when "Comes man, naked and mortal/Ready for truth, for speech, for wings."

54   *An oar over my shoulder, I walked from the woods*: The narrator is obviously in love with American Nature, which he duly romanticizes, as he did in his childhood when he read books for young people about travels in America. He also loves the way of life in rural parts of the United States, square dances, for instance. Observing one, he asks himself: why not stay in America for good? The temptation is strong, yet it takes its shape exclusively from the American countryside, not its cities. To live on a farm somewhere? It would mean to isolate oneself from the affairs of the twentieth century and from the political and philosophical commitments of Polish poetry.

55   *You will hear not one word spoken of the court/of Sigismund Augustus*: The reign of this king (1550–1572) was the golden age of Polish poetry. It was the time of Jan Kochanowski, whose play on a subject taken from Homer, *The Dismissal of the Greek Envoys*, was performed at court.

55   *Herodotus* (b. 484 B.C.) was, of course, the first European historian. Clio, goddess of history, is his muse.

55   *And the rose only, a sexual symbol*: For the narrator the option of staying in America for good would mean choosing life on its biological level. He was not the first European to feel in America the absence of historical memory, which is present at every step in Europe thanks to its architectural heritage. Though he admires American landscapes, he regards life in Nature as an impoverishment. What replaces history is sex, which becomes for people the main interest, the subject of their explorations. That is the meaning of the somewhat bizarre song on the interior of the rose.

56   *Let names of months mean only what they mean*: In some European countries the names of the months are associated with political events. October is the month of the Bolshevik Revolution in Russia, which was helped by the cannons of the ironclad ship *Aurora*. November for the Poles always suggests the 1830 uprising against tsarist Russia. It was begun by young rebels, officers stationed in Warsaw. The longing to forget these associations is the desire to renounce history.

57   *O October*: There is a sort of perversity in writing an ode to October simply as an autumn month, when historically it denotes the Russian Revolution, an event which had grave consequences for the whole twentieth century. The ode expresses the narrator's ecstatic enjoyment of the season and, undoubtedly, of his liberation from the fatal date in 1917.

57   *When a Polish engineer glimpses near West Point*: These lines suggest that he is, however, still in the grip of historical memories. The forests of New York recall to him the name of West Point and a Polish participant in the American revolution, Tadeusz Kościuszko (1746–1817), who built the fort's defenses.

58   *above the rebel camp*: Unmistakably the Poles who fought the Russians in 1863.

58   *You gave me the magic ring which, when turned,/Sends down a gleam from your jewel of freedom*: Does not our author, who was in the service of the Polish Embassy in Washington, D.C., from 1946 to 1950, reveal here conflicts of his own? The magic ring he wears is poetry. It is writing poetry that gives him a hidden sense of freedom.

58   *There is much with which to reproach us*: These lines testify to a decision already taken. The narrator has said "no" to a peaceful life on a farm somewhere in America, far from Poland and its insoluble problems. He is aware that this re-

fusal exposes his poetry to the turmoil of his times and precludes his use of it for the contemplation of "eternal truths." This passage repeats, in a concise form, the basic dilemma which confronts the narrator throughout the poem: poetry as contemplation of being or poetry as participation in movement, that is, in history, and thus a poetry of commitments? The first choice seems more in harmony with the vocation of the poet; the second involves a departure from the rules of a perfected art in the name of moral (?) passion.

58 *Neither the eternal moment/Attracted us*: The eternal moment is the opposite of time. It is, if only for a second, outside the flow of time. T. S. Eliot in *The Four Quartets* speaks of "the still point of the turning world." This idea often appears in the writings of mystics from various civilizations.

58 *nor purity of style*: The idea of purity as an essential trait of poetry preoccupied the French Symbolists of the second half of the nineteenth century—above all, Stéphane Mallarmé, who wanted to eliminate from his poems anything which was not necessary to its aesthetic purpose. In fact, he broke the link connecting a poem to reality, thus making a descriptive poetry impossible.

58 *We didn't care enough that they disappear*: Any actuality is short-lived, and art bound by it risks being forgotten. This poem is an example of radical opposition to "pure poetry" and of

its consequences. The poem is full of names and historical situations, and so, even for a Polish reader, the need for a commentary imposes itself.

59 *And yet the accusers were mistaken*: Who are the accused? Who are the accusers? Roughly speaking, the first are all those who have chosen movement, *devenir* or becoming, and accept therefore the flux of things, including the idea of truth. These are the disciples of Marx, Nietzsche, Dewey, etc. The narrator, despite his reservation about Marxism, belongs to this group. There are, however, people attached to a conservative vision of immutable essences. For them the partisans of flux and universal movement undermine, with their materialism and determinism, a divine order. This division into two camps has political implications. The peculiar situation of the author, who was not himself a Communist, but who was in the employ of a Communist government, exposed him to attacks from the political right. They are, perhaps, the accusers.

59 *There is no doubt that many perished, infamously*: A new, more mobile way of thinking is a dangerous tool, as is shown by the example of some people who, unprepared, read the subverters of traditional values, Nietzsche or Marx, and are tempted by the nihilist denial of Being, which to medieval thinkers was another name for God. The narrator advises against such an extreme; he wants to retain both ends of the contradiction. According to him, the observation of tangible things (the roundness of a stone, the gills of a

perch, a beaver) restores our reverence for the fundamental quality of the world, which is *esse*, "to be." Contemplation of that quality is a basic attribute, and the privilege, of poetry. Thus the narrator speaks here as a poet; he defends his craft against the encroachment of social and political duties. It seems to me that in his narrator's search for equilibrium the author has been influenced by American pragmatism, especially by William James's *Varieties of Religious Experience*, which he read in his early youth.

59 *For contemplation fades without resistance*: This line is directed against purity in poetry, but it is also a polemic with the T. S. Eliot of *The Four Quartets*. By renouncing the world for the sake of "the still point," of perfect stillness outside time, we may deprive contemplation of its intensity. Sugar is good, but it should not be eaten by the spoonful.

60 *And we, certainly, were happier than those/Who*: Here we are returned to the first part of the poem, to the time before the First World War when poets, isolated from society, rebelling against it but rejected by it, lived in garrets and read the philosopher most influential at that time, Arthur Schopenhauer (1788–1860). His pessimistic philosophy advocated a Buddhist nonattachment. He was one of the first European thinkers to borrow from the religions of India and through him the word "nirvana" entered the vocabulary of poets. This reception of Schopenhauer was, however, short-lived and limited to narrow circles of the literati. The author of the poem has been an admirer of the

philosopher, though he would find in him different things than did Schopenhauer's readers at the beginning of the twentieth century.

60   *At least poetry, philosophy, action were not, / For us, separated*: This is a bold statement, yet it is justified to some extent by the very fact of writing a work like *Treatise on Poetry*. It is, after all, a poem of commitment, both to a vision of what poetry should be and to a non-totalitarian model of society.

60   *If we, though our faults were merely historical, / Will not receive the laurel of long fame, / So what, after all?*: A considerable amount of humility is needed to make such a declaration. Hope for fame has always been a powerful motive for poets, and we may ask what makes the narrator willing to relinquish it. Perhaps he implies that the age of perfect art is over and that only an art aware of its lameness is possible? Anyway, he says, our lips "did not have time to say what they wanted."

60   *Spirits of the air, of fire, of water*: The last passage of the poem describes travel by ship to Europe in 1950. For the author, this was a very difficult option, slightly insane from a practical point of view, but not without a hidden existential logic. Staying in America, he might very well have written contemplative poetry, and he would probably not have produced prose like *The Captive Mind, Seizure of Power,* and *Native Realm,* books that arose from the circumstances to which he exposed himself: his feud with the Stalinists and

his life as an émigré. *A Treatise on Poetry,* written in France in 1955–56, traces a part of that journey. In succinct form, it explains why he could not, either philosophically or politically, be on the right, though he also rejected Communism. In that way, *Treatise* is about poetry as an all-embracing activity and not just an expression of personal feeling. It depicts the twentieth century not in general, but in one spot in Europe, Poland, where history took the guise of tragedy. It would be better, no doubt, to have chosen a less provincial topic. Yet there is a virtue to limiting a poem to the complexities one knows firsthand.

60 *Nothing but ocean which boils and repeats:/In vain, in vain*: The ocean is Nature and the frail ship, civilization.

61 *Iam Cytherea choros ducit Venus imminente luna*: Already Cytherean Venus leads choruses dancing under the rising moon.